Spearheading Growth

Spearheading Growth

How Europe's top companies are restructuring to win

Fritz Kröger
Michael Träm
Marianne Vandenbosch

FINANCIAL TIMES
PITMAN PUBLISHING

FINANCIAL TIMES
MANAGEMENT
LONDON · SAN FRANCISCO
KUALA LUMPUR · JOHANNESBURG

Financial Times Management delivers the knowledge, skills and understanding that enable students, managers and organisations to achieve their ambitions, whatever their needs, wherever they are.

London Office:
128 Long Acre, London WC2E 9AN
Tel: +44 (0)171 447 2000
Fax: +44 (0)171 240 5771
Website: www.ftmanagement.com

A Division of Financial Times Professional Limited

First published in Great Britain in 1998

© Financial Times Professional Limited 1998

The right of Dr Fritz Kröger, Dr Michael Träm and Marianne Vandenbosch to be identified as authors of this work has been asserted by them in accordance with the Copyright, Designs and Patents Act 1988.

ISBN 0 273 63772 X

British Library Cataloguing in Publication Data
A CIP catalogue record for this book can be obtained from the British Library.

All rights reserved; no part of this publication may be reproduced, stored in a retrieval system, or transmitted in any form or by any means, electronic, mechanical, photocopying, recording, or otherwise without either the prior written permission of the Publishers or a licence permitting restricted copying in the United Kingdom issued by the Copyright Licensing Agency Ltd, 90 Tottenham Court Road, London W1P 0LP. This book may not be lent, resold, hired out or otherwise disposed of by way of trade in any form of binding or cover other than that in which it is published, without the prior consent of the Publishers.

10 9 8 7 6 5 4 3 2 1

Typeset by Northern Phototypesetting Co Ltd, Bolton
Printed and bound in Great Britain by Biddles Ltd, Guildford and King's Lynn

The Publishers' policy is to use paper manufactured from sustainable forests.

About the authors

Dr Fritz Kröger has been working as a management consultant since 1976 in Europe, USA and Japan. His main expertise is in the field of strategy. As Vice President of A.T. Kearney in Germany, he co-chairs the Global Strategy Initiative of A.T. Kearney.

Dr Michael Träm is also Vice President at A.T. Kearney in Germany, focusing on strategy and restructuring. He has a background in law and much experience in consultancy projects throughout Europe. In particular, he leads M & A and post-merger integration projects.

Marianne Vandenbosch managed IMD's and A.T. Kearney's joint research project on the future of restructuring. Before coming to IMD, she lectured at the Richard Ivey School of Business (University of Western Ontario) in Canada.

Contents

Foreword by Percy Barnevik ix
Preface by Fred G. Steingraber xi
Acknowledgements xii

1 | Introduction:
Ready, steady, go – restructure for growth 1
Ready: Gear up for the challenge with a winning mindset 4
Steady: Find the strategy that will set you apart 7
Go: Make it happen. Again and again. 9

2 | Learning from experience:
What Europe's top companies have told us 13
The face of future restructuring 15
Lessons from the past 19
How the best differ from the rest 21

3 | A winning mindset:
Leader, Spearheaders and the organization 27
Lead the company's change in mindset 31
Challenge the enemies of a winning mindset 44
Foster a winning mindset 60

4 | Strategy demystified:
Focusing on essentials 85
Start with a vision 91
Set the strategy 97
Go for growth 116
Aim for relevance 126

5 Emphasis on action:
Turning strategy into reality 135

Let Spearheaders be your frontmen 138
Orient the stakeholders 139
Conduct for speed 149
Set and sustain the cadence of restructuring 156
Keep your eye on the ball 159

6 Towards the future:
There is one! 171

References 177

Index 179

Foreword

by Percy Barnevik
Chairman of ABB Ltd, Investor AB and Sandvik AB

Restructuring and restructuring again. This is one of the facts European companies have to face, and I am glad to say they are obviously able to accept this and act accordingly. It is also important to remember that, after restructuring and increased competitiveness, growth will follow. The broad example base of this book tells a story about what companies can do if they just try hard enough and never ever lean back in complacent self-esteem.

As a European manager with a personal history of restructurings and transformations, I can only recommend that you profit from lessons others have learned and dare to add your own experiences to company history.

Percy Barnevik

Preface

by Fred G. Steingraber, CEO A.T. Kearney, Chicago

One half millennium ago, one of the leaders of European Renaissance, whose work still inspires us, said that 'the noblest pleasure is the joy of understanding'.

Approaching the new millennium, as a new Europe emerges, the nimble and the able can look forward to a new form of Renaissance – an Economic Renaissance. For European companies the challenges are to anticipate change, take risks, seize opportunities, and indeed, to understand the implications of all that may lie ahead.

Engaged in a new competitivenesss, the best European companies are transforming themselves to operate globally, often spearheading growth through restructuring, reorganization and re-engineering and innovation. Renaissance requires leaders – leaders who understand that their number one responsibility is risk-taking. Without risk-taking, there is no change, and without change, there will be no growth or wealth creation.

In *Spearheading Growth*, the authors tap their consultancy experience to provide a lucid, clear view of the growth challenge ahead. Equally important, they write from the perspective of Europeans, offering the kinds of practical insights not often found in previous explorations of this subject.

On the pages that follow, leaders pursuing Economic Renaissance for their own companies will find valuable insights to improve their journey.

Acknowledgements

This is a book about company reality, and our insight into reality is again and again guided and deepened by our clients. So we would like to thank all our past and current clients, and also all participants in our recent restructuring survey and most of all, those companies and people who made it possible for us to gain an in-depth understanding about their restructuring success. These companies are Adtranz, Borealis, Deutsche Bahn AG, ELIN EBG, Fiat Auto and Hüls AG.

We are also grateful to the teams that supported us at A.T. Kearney and IMD, and also to Pradeep Jethi, our ambitious publisher at Financial Times Management.

Last but not least, a big 'thank you' to our editor, Dr Marianne Denk-Helmold, of A.T. Kearney for her knowledge, creativity, constructiveness and ability to keep cool. Without her, there would be no book.

Introduction

Ready, steady, go – restructure for growth

- *Ready:* Gear up for the challenge with a winning mindset.

- *Steady:* Find the strategy that will set you apart.

- *Go:* Make it happen. Again and again.

1 • Introduction

How do growth companies like BP, Unilever, Carrefour, Ahold or Roche do it? All too often the news in Europe is doom and gloom – stories of companies unable to compete with the overpowering North American juggernaut, of companies battered by the cost advantages in emerging markets. But these companies are thriving. Why? How?

Europe is the favourite topic of European business circles. 'Europe must do something.' 'Europe can't cling to its old ways.' 'The more we insist on doing things the same old way, the more we risk falling behind.' 'Europe can't just look to Europe any more.' 'European companies have to find ways to succeed in the *world*.' There is talk of the challenge of restructuring, of companies that have tried cutting costs and heads in a desperate attempt to move the business forward, but without much success. There is awe at North American progress. It moves steadily forward, conquering ever larger markets, and leaving European companies ever more vulnerable in a world of global competition.

> 'The more we insist on doing things the same old way, the more we risk falling behind.'

But back to the question at the beginning of this page. Some European companies demonstrate spectacular success, despite the *insurmountable* European problems that many try to hide behind. There is a way. And, more and more, there is a will. Despite the daily litany of troubled companies and failed restructurings, no day goes by without an announcement of new restructuring efforts. Choose any European newspaper, and the story is there.

It's the gap between these two realities – between those that are able to restructure, grow and succeed in a global economy, and those that try but fail, or those that don't even try – that captured our interest and led to this book.

We started with a European survey of restructuring. What had companies done in the past? What worked, what didn't work, and what led to disaster? What did the winners – the real success stories – do differently from the losers? And what are these same companies expecting to face in the future? More than 200 top managers of European companies across all industries shared their experiences with us in this survey. ('Us' is A.T. Kearney and IMD, the International Institute for Management Development, in Switzerland.)

As we presented the results of this survey throughout Europe, we created a Restructuring Affinity Council for business leaders who, like us, were interested in the tremendous potential as well as the persistent problems of restructuring. To date, we have held Affinity Council learning events in 13 European centres. The interactive sessions give industry leaders the chance to brainstorm on restructuring and to exchange their views on how to win in the world arena. And, unfailingly, they gave us food for thought in our reflections on restructuring.

We've pulled together the survey results, the Affinity Council discussions, and our firsthand experiences based on years of restructuring, to come up with our own proposal for how to make Europe win and close the gap between the glowing success stories, and the struggling and discouraged majority. It's time to leave the 'slash and burn' efforts of the past behind. It's time to treat restructuring as an opportunity to challenge new horizons and build value for employees and shareholders,rather than as a last resort to stave off bankruptcy. Now, how can we go about it for greater success?

Ready:

Gear up for the challenge with a winning mindset

Get everyone on the same team. Foster a can-do, pro-active outlook. Abandon inertia and complacency. For a lot of people, and for a lot of good reasons, restructuring is a dirty word – something to be avoided at any cost. At best, in their minds, it means change, which in itself isn't welcome to many. At worst, it means job loss and a very uncertain future. Launching a restructuring into that minefield could lead and often has led, to disastrous consequences.

Instead, it's important to nurture the right mindset before a restructuring gets underway. Dispel the concerns of employees before they get out of hand. *Management* understands that restructuring will be with us for the foreseeable future. It's important that everyone else in the company understands that too. The traditional view of restructuring – solving a big bad problem once or twice in a company's history – is out of date. Widespread deregulation, privatization and new market opportunities, coupled with more demanding customers and competitive invasions will force companies to adapt to new circumstances much more frequently. And those that can do so ahead of the problems and ahead of the pack will have a definite competitive edge. Make sure the whole company gets that whole picture. That turns restructuring from the big bad wolf into the knight in shining armour.

You want enthusiasm, not just acceptance. The more employees that buy into the company's potential, the more minds you have working to make sure that potential gets realized, no matter how many restructurings it takes. We look at both the enemies and the characteristics of a winning mindset, and we describe how to get rid of the former and nurture the latter.

First and foremost, it's a question of leadership. Leaders have to be believers, and they have to set good examples. They're the touchstone for the organization.

While your top executive is critical as the standard bearer for restructuring, you've got to remember there's only one of them. It'll take more than that to mobilize your whole company. You need a group of *Spearheaders*. A talented, dedicated, people-oriented team that can win over the hearts and minds of the rest of the organization and lead them through any and all restructuring challenges.

The mindset they need to foster is one that fights inertia, complacency, and arrogance. One that knows how to unearth new potential and anticipate needed change. Your company needs to be poised for action and filled with people that are results-oriented and willing to make decisions.

Choosing the Spearheading group carefully is an important start. As the Spearheaders go, so goes the restructuring. The Spearheaders then take up the mindset challenge.

They should encourage everyone to solicit the views of outsiders, to help foster an objective outlook and to unleash new perspectives. Sometimes those outsider viewpoints can exist even within your own company. Make sure you listen to those mavericks, whose points of view differ from the majority. They may be taking just the slant on things that will give your company the edge it seeks. If they're silenced too often for their out-of-the-ordinary views, they may stop offering them.

To succeed, the Spearheaders have to communicate like they've never communicated before. No matter where we looked, and no matter how vehemently management told us they knew communication was critical, when we hunted down the causes of restructuring problems and failures, communication was always one of the culprits. Lip service won't do the trick. They've got to communicate in a way that those they're communicating with find effective. That usually means much more frequent and much more detailed communication than anyone expects.

Spearheaders need confidence in the ability of the organization to get the job done, and they have to transmit that confidence to everyone else. The best way of doing that is to keep performance expectations high, and to reward achievement. A virtuous cycle of confidence/success/reward.

Finally, they've got to realize that shepherding mindset isn't a one-off job. They must pay attention to these issues all the time. What we're describing is a change in company culture, challenging the norms, solving problems and searching for opportunities. Developing people who want to embrace rather than shy away from restructuring and change. Cultural changes are profound, and need time to take root. The Spearheaders need to look for every opportunity to make the desired culture stick.

> **British Airways**
>
> Consider, for example, British Airways: freed from State ownership and tackling new markets, it now has the highest operating margins of any European airline. The first step was a complete turnaround of company culture. No longer were people working for British Airways because 'it's a job', and no longer were they ashamed to admit working there. Top management set the example, provided the training and encouraged its workforce to take their company's destiny into their own hands. By convincing the people of British Airways that the company had a great future and could be a great airline, top management tapped the energy and enthusiasm people had hidden, and directed it towards the company's goals.

Steady:

Find the strategy that will set you apart

Surprisingly, most companies keep strategy and restructuring separate. But those whose restructurings are driven by strategic needs outperform those whose restructurings are stopgap solutions to crises. Companies with a clear strategic focus achieve the best results most quickly.

Even more surprisingly, many companies stop short of really defining a strategy. We think that's a mistake. Without a strategy, every decision means a return to first principles. There's no filter, no context in which to evaluate what to do and what not to do. You'll invest a tremendous amount of energy to make sure your whole company is searching out opportunity and pulling in the same direction, so you've got to give them a direction to pull in. We're not talking about layers of strategic planning departments that take on a life of their own. We mean a real, implementation-oriented approach to figuring out what the company needs to look like to outpace its competitors and delight its customers for the next little while, and what changes it needs to get there.

We advocate boiling strategy down to the bare essentials. What will it take for us to outperform our competitors? What unique advantages can we offer our customers, and are there new customers and new packages of benefits we need to consider? To this end, we argue that there are really only two basic strategies to choose from: cost leadership, or a strategy of focus which distances you from your competitors through the package of benefits you offer your customers and potential customers. Your job is to choose which of those strategies brings you the most opportunity.

Finally, throughout Europe the refrain echoes, 'We need growth.' That's the one thing your strategy has to aim for above all else – profitable growth. Without growth you're unlikely to sustain the energy you've worked so hard to build. Growth gives you freedom to pursue the options that make most sense. This should make intuitive sense to any one of the thousands of companies that have been through a difficult downsizing, only to find out that at best they've managed to keep up with the competition, but more likely that soon they have to cut again.

> What unique advantages can we offer our customers, and are there new customers and new packages of benefits we need to consider?

Growth brings its own challenges. That's why it's best if it's planned rather than haphazard. Make sure you're ready to cope with the growth you're aiming at. And look for ways to grow with what you're good at.

Daimler-Benz

Daimler-Benz' difficulties in the recent past can be traced to its lack of focus. It chose an ambitious but diffuse strategy, and in that effort, diluted its resources. It wanted badly to grow, but chose to do so in areas in which it didn't have much expertise. After some initial success, the strain of operating in fields where it wasn't expert, and of spreading itself too thin dragged down the company's bottom line. Daimler-Benz can trace its recent turnaround directly to its decision to refocus on core businesses and core competencies: developing, assembling and marketing automobiles.

Go:

Make it happen. Again and again.

You've got the people on your side. You know what you want to accomplish. All that's left is the challenge of implementation. The combination of people, strategy, and action that makes the company's dreams come true.

Implementation is the domain of the Spearheaders. Their *raison d'être* is to make sure that the restructuring is a success. It's the job of the Spearheaders to articulate the strategy clearly and to translate it into a focused set of actions, complete with milestones and success measures.

Speed counts. That's a constant in our research, our discussions and our experience. Those that can restructure more quickly than their competitors win out time after time. They get the jump on their competitors and start to reap the benefits of restructuring more quickly. The improved results bring them added resources, making it easier to pursue new opportunities. A well-implemented restructuring gets even better if you can speed it up. That's our focus when we look at implementation: what you have to do to implement well and quickly. Not just once, but in every restructuring.

To minimize roadblocks, make sure your stakeholders are involved, informed and enthused. Not just your shareholders, not just your employees, but anyone who can have a significant impact on the restructuring you're carrying out. Your customers, for example. The workers' council. They need to be informed, and they need to believe there's something in the restructuring for them – otherwise, why support it?

Make decisions. And organize so that the turnaround time for decisions is always short. How? Make sure the Spearheaders understand the project and its time frame, and make sure the decision makers are always easily accessible. It's often better to make a decision quickly and without formality when it's really needed, than to wait for the formal process to grind slowly. The need for a decision – for action – often outweighs the benefits of a perfect, exhaustive analysis. As the old saying goes, it's better to be approximately right than exactly wrong.

The new restructuring reality is that once is not enough. Everyone we spoke to confirmed overwhelmingly that they expect to restructure repeatedly. That brings new challenges. What's the best way to run one restructuring after another? How can we avoid the restructuring burn-out that some have already noticed creeping into their workforces? How can you enable changes to take hold when the next set of changes starts before the current set is completely in place? Our answer to these new restructuring dilemmas? Plan the *cadence* of your restructuring efforts.

Cadence is the rhythm, the cycle of restructuring. Set a cycle that incorporates both the frenzy of activity during the restructuring and a period of calm thereafter. The period of calm lets the new systems, practices, and businesses take root. It gives breathing space to employees who can't indefinitely sustain the dual workload of restructuring and day-to-day activities. Setting that rhythm, that cadence, for your restructuring gives everyone the breaks they need. It's another important reason to restructure quickly. A speedy restructuring buys more time for the rest period you're trying to establish. You want time between the end of one restructuring project and the start of the next. You want a breathing space to reflect on opportunities for the next round of improvements. If you're always on the run, you have no time to think about where you should be running to.

Kvaerner

Kvaerner, the Norwegian shipbuilding, engineering and construction group, builds cadence into its restructuring efforts. On a consolidated level, there's virtually always some division of Kvaerner that's carrying out a restructuring. But the company is careful to make sure that each separate business gets breathing space between its restructurings. They're always evaluating possible acquisitions, but after each acquisition, they take time out to make sure the new enterprise has been successfully integrated, and to give everyone a break from the extra effort that entails.

We outline what we think is the best way to ensure your restructuring succeeds. We base it on what we, and hundreds of executives throughout Europe, see works and doesn't work. We pay special attention to those who have succeeded, learning what it takes to do it right. In a nutshell, the best restructurers are committed, fast and focused. We've looked behind those traits to see how they can be encouraged within an organization, and encapsulated them as concepts you can apply in your next restructuring.

We challenge top executives throughout Europe to conduct a review of their own strategy and operations. Have you already identified the challenges that will shape the future? Has the firm taken the right moves to address them? Can the company turn the strategy into reality? How will your company adapt to the need to restructure repeatedly? Working through the concepts in this book, and comparing what is going on in your firm to the ideal situation, will almost certainly yield striking directions for improvement. And if you follow those directions, you'll be that much closer to becoming one of Europe's winners, and to making Europe win.

> **We outline what we think is the best way to ensure your restructuring succeeds.**

2

Learning from experience

....

What Europe's top companies have told us

■ The face of future restructuring

■ Lessons from the past

■ How the best differ from the rest

A rich source of information for the ideas we present in this book was the in-depth restructuring survey we carried out with European executives from companies such as Ansaldo, AGIV, BASF, Bayer, Du Pont de Nemours, Fiat, Philip Morris Europe, Thyssen, VEBA, etc. IMD and A.T. Kearney collaborated on this survey to better understand the tricks and trends that have shaped restructuring, and more importantly, those that will shape it in the future. What can companies do to improve a troubled track record? Can they learn from those who have succeeded before them? Which mistakes are most likely, and how can they be avoided in the future? And what do executives expect the future will hold in terms of restructuring?

> **What can companies do to improve a troubled track record?**

The survey gave us access to the opinions and experiences of top European companies across a broad range of industries. We gathered 211 responses, with strong representation from top executives of large firms.

The face of future restructuring

Frequent

The days of restructuring as a one-time adjustment are over. Survey respondents were almost unanimous: 90% of them expect to run an on-going stream of restructuring projects in their business units over the next ten years (see Figure 2.1).

These statistics suggest three things. First, management is finally starting to see restructuring as a pro-active measure instead of a reaction to an emergency situation. Second, companies will finally have to outgrow the 'slash and burn' mentality that overwhelmed past restructuring. Companies simply won't be able to aggressively

Spearheading Growth

cut costs and people on a continuous basis over ten years. Finally, the need to restructure to stay competitive outweighs concerns about past restructuring failures. Quite clearly, executives have chosen restructuring as the way to meet the challenges of the future.

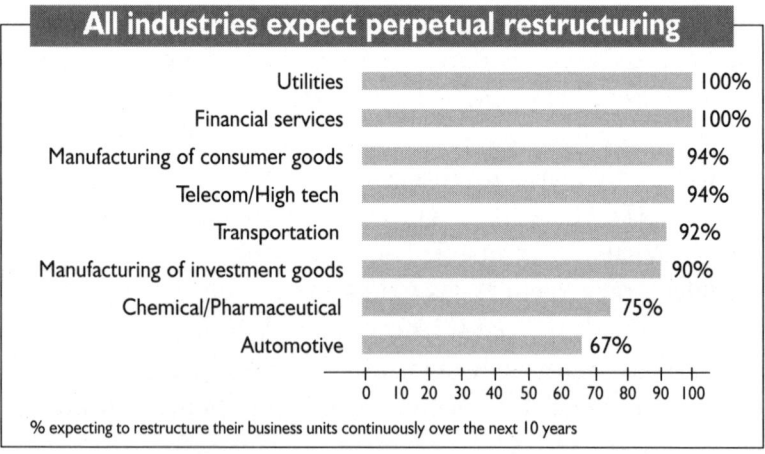

Figure 2.1

Global

What will that restructuring be addressing? All industries but utilities named *globalization* as the biggest restructuring challenge they expect to face in the future (see Figure 2.2).

2 • Learning from experience

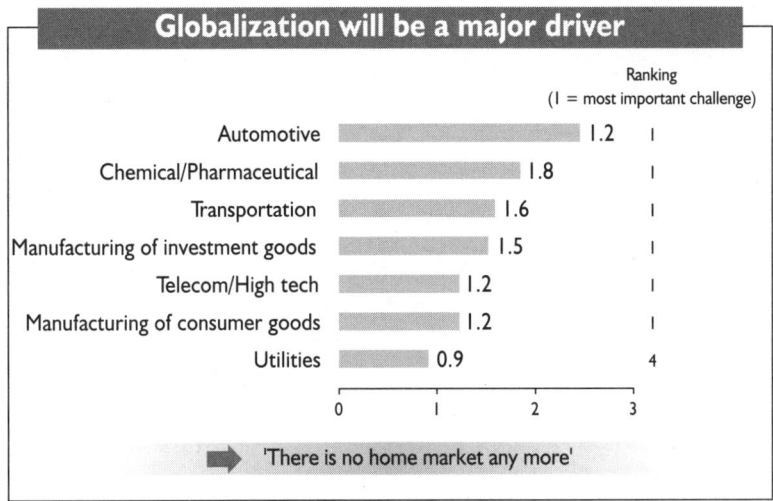

Figure 2.2

The automotive industry, arguably one of the most globalized, stands out from the rest. It gives significantly more weight to globalization than other industries. Perhaps because they are so experienced in globalizing, those in the auto industry realize better than others what a tremendous challenge it can be. Or perhaps their experience has shown them that the benefits of globalization are so great that they want to place even more emphasis on it in the future. In any case, Europe's executives have clearly recognized that they'll have to look beyond Europe's borders in the future. As one of the survey respondents so eloquently put it: *'There is no home market any more.'*

Interdependent

Other borders will be blurring in the future as well: those between companies. A growing number of companies expect to forge alliances. Acquisitions, joint ventures and development of joint competencies with suppliers and customers are all expected to increase in frequency in the future. Here is a spectacular example for how well this can work from the Nordic region:

Spearheading Growth

> ### Borealis
>
> Borealis A/S was formed in 1994 with the merger of the polyolefins divisions of the Norwegian oil company Statoil and its Finnish counterpart, Nesté. The polyolefins industry is cyclical, with narrow profit margins and commodity-like price fluctuations. In an industry with too many small players, Borealis emerged as the largest producer in Europe, and the 5th largest worldwide. That was the first step. Borealis demonstrates the move towards more alliance and joint-venture-related activities, as identified in our survey. In its quest to improve profits and cement customer relationships, Borealis has developed close partnership-type relationships with core customers and suppliers. Each core customer combines its expertise in marketing, technology and logistics with a corresponding cross-functional team from Borealis. The same principle has been applied with suppliers, producing major savings for both. In mid-1997, Borealis reported a group operating profit of ECU 118 million up sharply from ECU 24 million for the first half of 1996, and the strong customer and supplier relationships played a big role in the improvement.

This success story is particularly striking in the light of failure rates as high as 2 in 3 for mergers and acquisitions in the recent past. The challenge of globalization will be met, at least in part, through alliances, joint ventures and other forms of partnering (Figure 2.3).

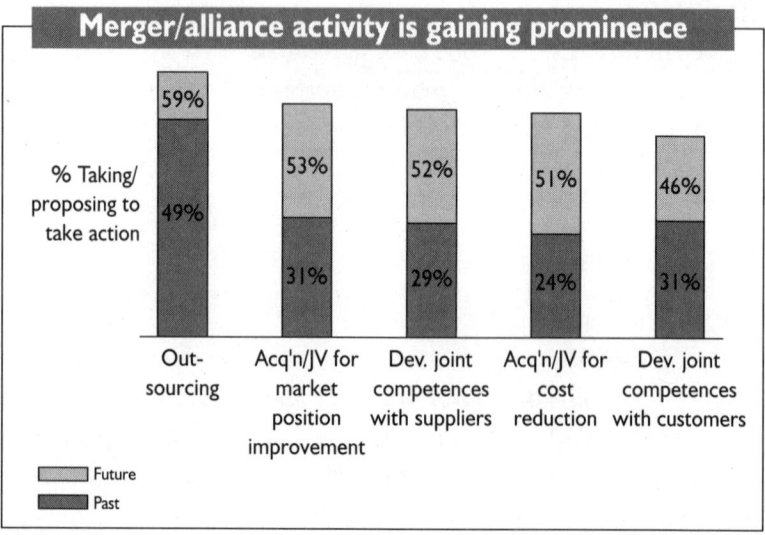

Figure 2.3

2 • Learning from experience

This increase in alliances could conceivably create competition for good partners. It will be ever more important to consider how to identify good alliance partners, and how a company can make itself attractive as an alliance partner. You want to choose a good partner, and you want a good partner to choose you. After all, a bad alliance could be worse than none at all.

Lessons from the past

The survey gave us the luxury of being able to stand back and look at the big picture. The chance to read between the lines to see what people were telling us beyond the words they put on their page. What did we find? In short, actions speak louder than words.

The vast majority of restructuring obstacles described by survey respondents related to people issues (see Figure 2.4).

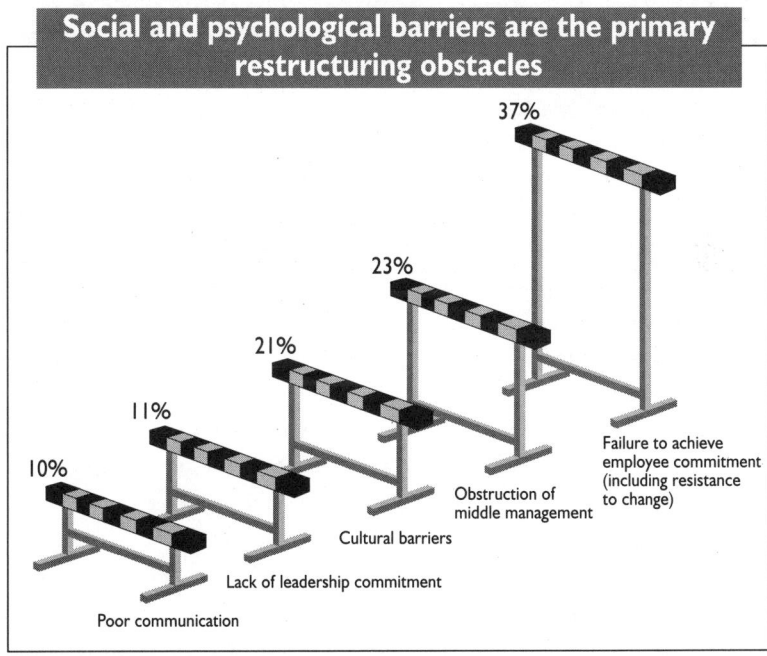

Figure 2.4

Spearheading Growth

There's no doubt about it, getting the people issues right is critical. But despite the fact that most companies name employees as a vital restructuring success factor (second only to top management commitment), most have a hard time getting it right. One of the reasons may well be that they don't follow through on their stated belief in the importance of employees.

These survey findings corroborate what we see everyday. Employees are always *said* to be important, but top management doesn't back that statement up with action. And thinking back to the barriers, the difficulties with top management commitment and lack of communication were essentially self-assessment by senior management. The problem could have been much bigger if we asked opinions further down the organization.

ELIN EBG

For newly merged companies, successful post-merger integration is absolutely critical. The Austrian ELIN EBG, formed out of ELIN Energieanwendung and Elektro Bau AG is a success story in that department. The new ELIN EBG is now the leading Austrian player for customer specific electrotechnical and electronic systems, plants and services.

Four key steps that helped them achieve success were:

1. An interim organizational structure was in place the day the merger was announced. Mergers cause uncertainty, and people (customers, suppliers, lenders and employees) all wonder what the merger means for them and how it will work. By having the organizational structure decided at the time of the merger announcement, a lot of those questions can be answered almost before they're asked.
2. Key personnel were in place for the top two organizational levels at the time of the merger anouncement. Again, ELIN acted to make sure it had a real company in place right away. There weren't just cold empty boxes on an organizational chart, waiting to be filled in. The people were there, ready to move forward in the merged organization, and ready to answer questions for everyone else involved in the merger.
3. A key account management strategy was put into place immediately. One of the parties most significantly affected in a merger is the customer. Often a customer waits for information (or goes elsewhere) while a company is struggling to sort out its internal processes. ELIN EBG made

> sure that its customers had no concerns, and no reason to go elsewhere, by contacting all key customers immediately after the merger announcement. Customers were never in doubt as to whom they should deal with or how they would fare as a result of the merger.
> 4 A preliminary business plan for the merged company was quickly devised. Again, ELIN EBG acted quickly and decisively to make sure that the synergies it expected from the merger would be realized.
>
> Often, companies breathe a sigh of relief at the end of merger negotiations, and forget that the hard work starts the day the deal is signed. The two companies which merged to form ELIN EBG attribute part of their success to the careful attention they paid to post-merger issues, and to their understanding that announcing a merger was not nearly enough to make sure the merger would work.

Our observation out of all of this: management skill in handling the soft side of restructuring could become a competitive advantage. Companies that handle the people issues well will be able to run better, smoother and faster restructuring projects than less people-oriented competitors.

The other big lesson from the past is that it's hard to shake the cost-orientation underlying most past restructuring. No matter what the respondents told us was the purpose of the restructuring, the same old performance measures surfaced time and time again. How much were costs reduced? How many employees did we get rid of? What happened to the productivity numbers? They're all relevant questions, but asking only those to the exclusion of others, means that those are the issues people will address. If the measures are purely cost-driven, it's tough to get people to think at all about conquering new markets.

How the best differ from the rest

Here's where we spent most of our time sifting through the survey data. Why were some companies able to improve their results by 70% (pre- to post-restructuring), while others limped along? Just

Spearheading Growth

> **Why were some companies able to improve their results by 70% (pre- to post-restructuring), while others limped along?**

under 10% of those who took part in the survey – our top performers – were able to achieve those results, and we found some telling differences between these stars and the rest of the restructurers.

Faster, higher, stronger

The companies with the best results restructured more quickly ('faster'); were more growth-oriented ('higher'); and had a stronger strategy emphasis and stronger focus than those they outperformed ('stronger').

Speed

Top performers spent less time on all phases of restructuring, and on average managed to restructure in 30% less time than their less successful counterparts.

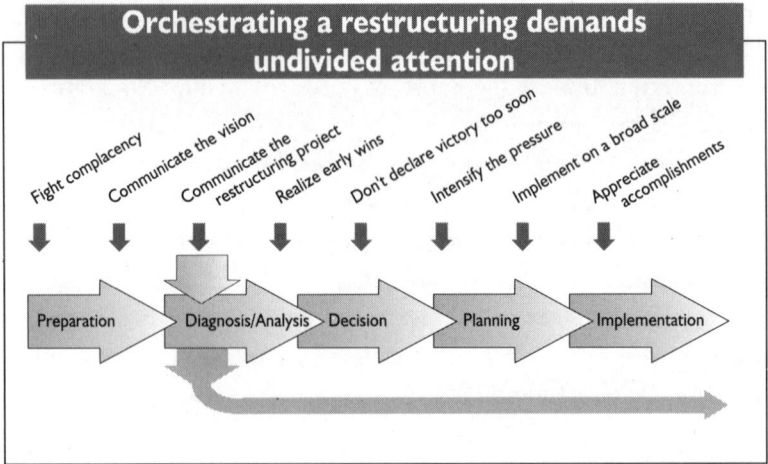

Figure 2.5

A speedy restructuring keeps people enthused, provides improved results faster, and gives you the jump on slower competitors.

> **Unilever**
>
> Niall FitzGerald, chairman of Unilever, is showing his company and the stock markets how to benefit from speeding up restructuring. He took over as chairman in September 1996, determined to speed up the process of refocusing Unilever on its key businesses, and immediately divesting those that didn't fit into core categories. Under FitzGerald, the refocusing has picked up speed. Analysts comment that Unilever is indeed leaner and more focused. Unilever's cash cushion at the end of 1997, about ECU 5 billion, has also drawn comments: 'This is the reward of restructuring – the extra cash to help kick-start new business,' Richard Newboult, an analyst at Lehman Brothers in London, told *Wall Street Journal* in February 1998.

How do fast companies differ from slower ones? Survey results showed focus was a key differentiator between those who accomplished restructuring quickly and those who took a long time. And slow restructurers tend to concentrate on developing competencies internally; those who restructured quickly acquired the needed competencies externally. Patterns of employee involvement also differed markedly between the two groups.

As we've already pointed out, getting employee involvement right is a big deal. So what did the fast restructurers do? They had relatively high involvement of employees in the early, problem definition and option generation phases of restructuring, virtually no involvement in making decisions on what course of action to take; and a fairly high level of involvement in implementing the restructuring solution. In contrast, slow restructurers had little employee involvement in the first phases of restructuring. Message? It's easier to gain buy-in early in the process. If employees have helped to identify problems they are more likely to be committed to implementing solutions to those problems.

Focus

Top performers were more focused than the rest. When asked about the importance of focus on core business to the success of restructuring, top performers gave it almost three times as much weight as those who were less successful.

And those who restructured quickly took fewer actions, considered fewer stakeholders and focused on fewer performance measures. In other words, they clearly defined what they wanted to accomplish, and didn't let themselves get distracted along the way.

Just what have leading edge companies been focusing on? Their restructuring efforts were more growth-oriented than those of their less successful counterparts. New market opportunities were 3.5 times more important to top performers. Breakthrough business expansion, globalization and the need to get larger were twice as important to the leaders as they were to the rest. They were more likely to enter into acquisitions or joint ventures, and to enter new markets. And they were less likely to close capacity. Although cost is and will remain a key issue for most, leading edge companies realize that they can't save themselves into prosperity.

The focus on growth demonstrates a strategic approach to restructuring. Those with poorer results were more likely to take actions that were less strategy-related, such as reducing the workforce or implementing an IT system. The choice is between short-term 'fix it for now' or 'buying time' projects and the development of a longer-term strategic direction for a company. The longer-term perspective wins in this survey.

New management

There's one more piece to the puzzle. Top performers had a stronger emphasis on a change in ownership or management than did the rest of the companies surveyed.

Of the top performing companies, 75% had a change in ownership or management before their restructuring, as opposed to only 32% in the rest of the sample (see Figure 2.6). That certainly doesn't mean that existing management can't successfully re-invent their companies or redefine their industries, but it does mean that they should be thinking about what new management brings to the table.

> Top performers had a stronger emphasis on a change in ownership or management than did the rest of the companies surveyed.

2 • Learning from experience

New management helps open the company's eyes

```
75%                    Implications of new management
                        • Fresh vision
                        • No sacred cows
   Top                  • Organization expects change
   perfor-              • Experience from other companies
   mers
                        32%

                        The
                        rest
```
% with new ownership or management before restructuring

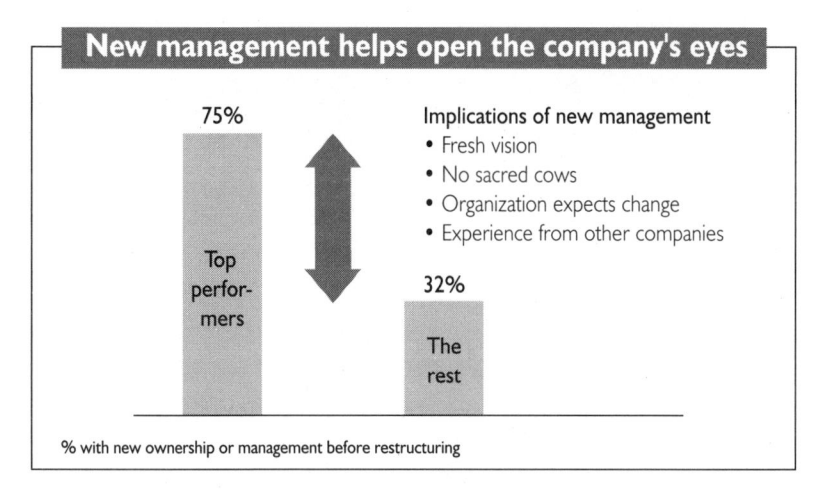

Figure 2.6

Based on our survey results, the overwhelming conclusion is that the difference between the people that are really good at restructuring and everybody else is that they live it. It takes dedication. It takes decisions when some would prefer delay. It takes what the top performers showed – the ability to get things done.

3

A winning mindset

Leader, Spearheaders and the organization

- Lead the company's change in mindset
- Challenge the enemies of a winning mindset
- Foster a winning mindset

'It was difficult to convince employees that a new culture was needed for survival'

'Personal agendas and insecurities were our biggest obstacles'

'Good business results were our biggest barrier to change'

3 • A winning mindset

Most of the roadblocks companies hit in their restructurings are 'people problems', and 'mindset' issues. Restructurings flounder because people don't fully commit themselves, because they don't see the need for restructuring, because they can't break out of their old ways, or because the restructuring just lacks leadership.

The biggest obstacle to restructuring is employee resistance, especially at the middle management level. That's partly because of the widespread history of 'slash and burn' restructurings. Faced with a restructuring that could leave them jobless, resistance looks like a sensible option. And when they have been the main victims of brutal cost-cutting and downsizing, it's no surprise that employees and middle management want nothing to do with the next round. But fear isn't the only reason it's hard to turn employees into keen restructurers. Inertia and complacency also play a role. It's simply easier for them to do what they've always done – especially when it has been done well. To break from that tradition, they'll have to recognize that clinging to the *status quo* could lead to ruin.

> **Leadership commitment is essential to successful restructuring.**

Cultural barriers also impede restructuring. Changing a culture is difficult, because it means changing how people think about themselves. Complications grow when merging two different business cultures, or two different ethnic cultures: people want to defend their turf against invaders. In future, cultural barriers may grow even greater. More mergers and alliances, and more globalization, will push more and more companies into situations where two cultures need grafting into one.

Leadership commitment is essential to successful restructuring. If the leaders don't have their act together, the followers can't get anywhere either. If the leaders aren't fully behind the restructuring, the resources and attention needed are usually also lacking, and the restructuring suffers.

> **AEG**
>
> Take the example of AEG, a grand old German company with more than 150 years of history. Its closure in 1996 was a direct result of management's inability to decide on and stick to a clear and coherent course of action for the company. First problems emerged in the early 1970s, but top management's efforts to restructure were half-hearted and failed. They weren't clear about what needed to be done and showed no commitment to the process. As a result, middle management blocked the improvements. That was the beginning of a long slow death.

Focused and committed leadership provides the rudder for a restructuring – without that guidance, restructuring can easily stray off course. But – let's face it – there is an immense gap between the leaders and their employees – a gap that needs to be bridged. A group of Spearheaders, drawn together from throughout the organization, can provide that bridge. There are two good reasons why Spearheaders are an important part of successful restructurings:

- *Reason 1:* Their involvement helps them see the project from a different angle and this new perspective will make them support the project.
- *Reason 2:* There has to be a closely knit web supporting top management and at the same time addressing operational level employees in a language they understand.

Poor communication completes the list of top restructuring obstacles. It underlies most other problems. If middle management resists, or if employees aren't supportive, it's often because they haven't been adequately involved, or feel they don't know what's going on. Cultural barriers can only be broken down through communication and interaction. Wishing them away won't work. The amount of effort it takes to get everyone into the same boat and rowing in the same direction is very often underestimated, making the restructuring voyage much rougher than it needs to be.

3 • A winning mindset

> **Communication problems**
>
> In anticipation of a merger between two electrical engineering competitors, and realizing that employees would have lots of questions, top management of one of the companies put together an extensive communication package. It was professionally designed and delivered by a public relations agency, and it addressed the issues that top management felt might be of concern. Top management was very proud of its foresight and effort. They were shocked to learn, when carrying out independent checks, that despite extensive communication most employees felt that they didn't know what was going on; that they were being kept in the dark.

Communication gets to be a problem because it's easy to be lulled into thinking that you've done what's needed. That's a one-sided view. You've only done what's needed when the people you're interacting with feel that you have.

What's the common thread through all these obstacles? People's reluctance to throw themselves with vigour into renewing their companies. It's tough to work on something you don't believe in. It's tough to restructure when you don't think it's necessary. It's tough to see potential when you're content with what you have.

If you want to get the most out of your restructuring, shake loose lethargy and ignite energy and creativity. Develop a winning mindset – throughout the organization. An open-minded, hard-working, can-do mindset really is the foundation of a successful restructuring. Restructuring demands commitment, hard work, tenacity and forward thinking. If you're just going through the motions, your company will fall short of its potential.

Lead the company's change in mindset

'The enemy of any restructuring is senior managers who resist change'

There's almost no way to separate a leader from the success or failure of the entity he or she leads. Look at how quickly Britain's

Conservative party replaced John Major after their crushing election defeat. And who takes the fall for a losing football team? It's more likely to be the manager than the players. The same applies in business – whether you like it or not, as a leader you are on the hot seat. If people don't buy in, it's a leadership issue: an inability to communicate and motivate, or an inability to select the right people. If competitors steal market share it's a leadership issue: failure to read evolving market conditions, or complacency, or an inability to mobilize the organization quickly enough. Leaders have to face the fact that any serious company problem will be attributed, at least in part, to them.

It sounds heavy-duty, but that responsibility is warranted. Think about it. There's no one else who has the same power over, and therefore ability to influence, everyone in the company. Leaders make a big difference in almost any aspect of a business. They can make all the decisions themselves, or they can encourage the development of their people. They can search out new ideas, or guard the *status quo*. The choices a leader makes, and the approaches he takes, will shape the organization's mindset – and the company's success often does reflect the leader's work. That becomes even clearer when you consider how unlikely it is for a company to achieve great things with an ineffective leader.

In restructuring, the chances of success without strong leadership are even more remote. In a steady state situation, a company with strong systems and well-trained people can sustain its operations for a time. But restructuring challenges that steady state. It challenges the way we do business and the business we're in. Instead of asking people to perfect what they've always done, we ask everyone to break out of past patterns and comfort zones. Companies and people will cling to those comfort zones without some prodding to let go, and top management initiates that prodding. If they are satisfied with the *status quo*, like the majority of managers and employees in Western and Central Europe, there's very little impetus for anyone in the organization to change.

Provide strong role models

'This restructuring was a flop because top management did not "walk the talk"'

A genuine leader is one who really lives his leadership. He honours the privilege of leadership by refusing to take it for granted. His vision and focus and determination come from the heart. That means really developing contact with and understanding your people, and being open to what you learn through those contacts. A genuine leader is a guide, a listener, a supporter, a visionary, a provider of perspective, and a decision-maker.

> **When a company restructures, top management is in the spotlight.**

Leaders set the tone. When a company restructures, top management is in the spotlight. You deliver messages in two ways: you *say* what they stand for and support, and your actions *show* how deeply your commitment actually runs. Everyone looks to the leader to learn the new priorities, whatever they may be.

'If you look only – or consistently first – at financial results, so will your people, at all levels. But if you focus instead on quality of product or customer service, or growth, or new markets or innovation, your people will follow your lead.'[1]

To become a genuine leader you have to be absolutely consistent between what you say and what you do. The messages you deliver must ring true. In restructuring, because it means change, that heartfelt consistency is even more important. When trying to foster change, when trying to get people looking where they haven't looked before and in ways they haven't thought about before, your example as a leader is critical.

To deliver that consistency in thought and deed, leaders need to be believers themselves. You must embrace the need for change, and feel it deep down in your bones. Like the people you lead, you will find it a challenge to leave behind what you have built. That's a special difficulty faced by a company's existing management –

new management would have no ties to the good old days. And even those who are able to *say* change is needed, will find *living* that change difficult.

> *'Perhaps the most significant resistance to change comes from the fact that leaders have to indict their own past decisions and behaviours to bring about change ... Psychologically it is very difficult for people to change when they were party to creating the problems they are trying to change.'*[2]

To get around that difficulty, look ahead, not back. Restructuring reflects the changes the company needs to succeed in changed circumstances, not the need to fix past wrongs. You're looking for ways to get an edge and you need to learn new habits, not because you were wrong before, but because something different is needed now.

Leading by example happens whether you want it to or not.

Bertelsmann

Bertelsmann, the world's largest media enterprise, is a living example of the positive impact a leader can have on his company. Under Mark Wössner's leadership the company has changed from a staid, conservative enterprise to a shooting star in the industry. A company where young up-and-comers are keen to work. Wössner's forward-looking, assured and charismatic approach shows up throughout the company. Not because he has ordered it, but because people have taken their cue from him.

Employees will jump on inconsistencies as a reason to do nothing, or to fall back into the comfortable cocoon you're trying to drag them out of. You need to be unwavering. The messages you deliver should fit together, and the actions you take should match the messages. Without question, you are the ultimate role model. If you're consistent, your people will build on the example you set. If you're not consistent, you'll still be a role model, but one which people can twist to suit their own purposes – justification for falling back into old ways.

Restructuring runs into trouble when 'top management doesn't walk the talk'. Think about the trouble you had getting people on board in your last initiative. Were you part of the problem? Were you sending mixed messages? Challenge yourself to see whether you got caught in any of these traps (see Figure 3.1).

Leader says	Leader does
You people are our most important resource	Begin restructuring by announcing headcount reduction
We want all your good ideas and help to carry us to our next level of success	Issue a company strategy and implementation plan without having consulted anyone except top management team
Our most important task is to create value for the customer: in the long run that will bring us healthy sales	Demand that specific bottom line targets are met, no matter what it takes to do so
We've got to learn new skills	Limit funds or time available for training in new skills
We want to open the communication lines in both directions	Make himself inaccessible to employees, and communicate by newsletter only
We've got to take some chances if we want a real breakthrough	Punish the slightest failure
Teamwork is essential	Reward individual performance

Figure 3.1

As the saying goes, actions speak louder than words. A leader's focus on the bottom line will be mirrored by his people, even if ten newsletters go out urging everyone to concentrate on the customer. The CEO who takes a pay cut and travels economy class will gain more support for a belt-tightening initiative than the one who gets a raise while employees are losing jobs. No matter what you *say*, others will listen more to what you *do*.

Spearheading Growth

> ### Elf Aquitaine
>
> Early in his tenure, Philippe Jaffré, the unconventional CEO of Elf Aquitaine, demonstrated his willingness to live his example. Jaffré and thirty of his senior managers were graduates of the École Nationale d'Administration (ENA) in France, known as *énarques*. ENA graduates are guaranteed jobs and pensions within the civil service for life. They regularly take periods of employment with State-owned companies. Jaffré's job was to privatize Elf, and he forced his senior managers to choose between a career with Elf or the right to keep their privileges as *énarques*.
>
> 'Jaffré's demand provoked outcry in the upper echelons of the civil service, but all Elf employees chose to stay with him. "It did prompt a bit of a revolt among civil servants," admits Jaffré, but he insists that taking the moral high ground has paid off. "In your work as a manager, you have to fire people, so how can you look people in the eye if, as an *énarque*, you yourself are safe from unemployment? We needed to make sure we were in the same boat as all other Elf employees."'[3]

Philippe Jaffré realized that *we* may judge ourselves by our intentions, but others will certainly judge us by our behaviour. Good leaders encourage feedback. Tell your people you want to be challenged. You want them to pressure you to live up to your ideals. And when someone points out that you've slipped up, don't shoot the messenger – change your behaviour. As Jan Leschly, CEO of SmithKline Beecham, the winning pharmaceutical company that has averaged over 10 million ECU in turnover and 1.5 million ECU in profit, says so succinctly:

> '*I don't want anyone around who will mindlessly echo what I think is right or wrong*'[4]

Be broad-minded, balanced and decisive

> '*Our new emerging culture is more active and client oriented, especially in operating units*'

3 • A winning mindset

Over the next ten years, 90% of European executives are expecting to restructure their business units continuously. Everyone expects the pressure for change to be relentless, and they see restructuring as the way to achieve that change. Leaders need a broad perspective and a great capacity to absorb and simplify complexity in order to meet the challenge of repeatedly restructuring while at the same time running the day-to-day business. It's clear that dual role will become a required competency for most CEOs. CEOs also need the objectivity to see when change is needed and when it's best to stay the course. It's one thing to develop a change-ready organization, but it's another thing to urge change even when none is needed. When you race from change to change you may not stand still long enough to collect the benefits of one change before you leap to a new one.

Strong leaders choose change for impact, not for fashion. If you do not understand the competitive environment in which your company operates, you won't be able to identify when change is needed and what the most appropriate change is. You won't be able to guide your people to the right activities and ensure that they have the right skills.

Leaders face conflict and contradiction. A good leader fits his approach to the situation. At times the tough authoritarian, at times the supportive cheerleader. The results-oriented and very focused field marshal, the wild-eyed inventor who believes all is possible. The yin and yang – capable of seeing the whole picture, not just part of it. The ability to see the forest and the trees, and to know when to focus on each. One of the most important balancing acts is between the pressures of day-to-day management and restructuring. If one or the other is over-emphasized, the company won't be able to meet its goals. You need to get rid of thinking that accepts the situation where *'restructuring was a problem because it caused disruption to our business-as-usual processes'*.

Strong leaders feel the pulse of their company because they frequently talk to people all over the organization. They assess emerging pressures (both internal and external) because they have enough knowledge and experience to do so. They have the courage to make tough decisions. Participants in our restructuring

Affinity Council feel that the necessary decision-making courage is often lacking. They pointed out that top management in general is too slow in making decisions throughout restructuring because they fear the consequences of those decisions, and that the absence of strong leaders willing to make choices impedes the development of strategy. The message from the Affinity Council is certain: a successful restructuring demands leaders who are, first and foremost, decision-makers.

Being the ultimate decision-maker, however, doesn't mean you sit in the executive suite and send out decrees. The leader is the one with the broad perspective, but those with narrower perspective can also have a deeper understanding. You should get lots of input from the insights of others in the organization. It would be crazy to use the brain power of your people only to do what you told them. You want to know what they think as well. You want their whole brains, not just the obedient parts.

So – especially in a critical restructuring situation – effective leadership cannot flourish in isolation. As the leading person or one of the leading people you have to make sure that you do not lose contact with the crowd and that you can rely on a large group of people who not only give you feedback and open criticism but also support your restructuring project.

Encourage Spearheaders to draw people together and pay attention to detail

'It worked so well because we integrated and empowered middle management to a larger extent than ever before'

Leaders are the foundation of any restructuring, and they play a vital public relations role during the entire transformation. The restructuring survey identified them as the most important restructuring success factor. An equally critical role for top executives is the selection of Spearheaders to guide the restructuring. The lengthy list of people problems that cripple most restructuring efforts sends a powerful message: restructuring needs Spearheaders to draw people together and propel the firm successfully into the future.

Furthermore, the simultaneous demands of day-to-day operations and restructuring stretch top management to its limits. No CEO, no matter how charismatic, no matter how energetic, can lead the restructuring alone. Restructuring which depends on only one leader or on only a top management group, risks spreading people too thin, and not capitalizing on beneficial relationships that have developed within the organization. Restructuring takes lots of time and attention to detail, and a well-chosen Spearheading Team can provide that, thus multiplying top management's energy and vision.

Let the Spearheaders set the pace

The Spearheaders lead the rest of the organization through the restructuring. They act as leaders, but need not be the top level of the traditional functional hierarchy. They are the dedicated group of people who can be counted on to understand what needs to be done, to cut across organizational boundaries as required, to get the message across to others, and to finish what they start.

The responsibility of the restructuring Spearheaders is to mobilize the rest of the organization and drive the restructuring. The Spearheaders make the restructuring happen. Cascading the restructuring through the organization, fostering new thinking and new spirit, spotting and resolving problems early. They are the linchpin between top management and the rest of the organization.

Spearheaders fill a number of roles. They will work with the organization to chart the exact course of the restructuring. There's no doubt that the Spearheaders should be working *with* the rest of the organization, not smoothing the way for them. The goal is an organization in which everyone is active – looking for new and better ways, not just following a trail blazer. Spearheaders are an innovative, devoted group with a willingness to flout hierarchy and concentrate on getting things done. A team that's respected and trusted on all levels of the hierarchy and has the energy, vision and dedication to help the organization through the restructuring. The challenge of nurturing a winning mindset, the challenge of getting the restructuring accomplished – this is the work of the Spearheaders.

Target, train and motivate achievers for the Spearheading team

The group needs to have the resources, skills and mandate to drive and achieve the restructuring. Selecting the appropriate team requires a good understanding of the interpersonal dynamics in the company. Identify and evaluate existing power coalitions – what will it take to make them committed restructurers? Who will be able to win over influential groups? The team need not, and should not, be composed only of people in the upper layers of the hierarchy. To foster a pro-active, thinking and committed mindset, the Spearheaders benefit from people at various levels in the organization.

> Selecting the appropriate team requires a good understanding of the interpersonal dynamics in the company.

Figure 3.2 shows the five key characteristics that each team of Spearheaders needs in order to be able to fulfil its mandate: functional leadership, position power, credibility, experience and future perspective. These will give the Spearheaders the power base – the formal, and more importantly, informal, authority they need to work effectively within the company and accomplish the restructuring. The search is not for superhumans that each have all five characteristics, but rather for a team of talented people that combine these traits.

The position power member is someone with hierarchical authority. As the CEO/ chairman/managing director you should take this role. It is further proof of your commitment to the restructuring, and it solves the problem of rapid access to senior management for decision-making that plagues many restructurings. Whoever takes on this role, however, should remember that the hierarchical power they bring to the group is to lend it credibility with the company as a whole, not within the team. The position power member has to be careful not to wield his power too aggressively within the Spearheading team, in order not to stifle other members.

The kind of 'expert' the team needs is usually evident once some preliminary direction for the restructuring is fixed. The expert provides depth of knowledge in an important area of the restructuring. Since the Spearheading team effects the restructuring, they must have the appropriate resources and expertise to be able to lead the rest of the organization. They must have the knowledge needed to make appropriate decisions regarding the restructuring, for example about organizational principles or information needs. But it's even more critical for the way the rest of the organization views the Spearheaders. If a restructuring involves entering some new markets, for example, and there's no one on the Spearheading team with marketing experience, the rest of the organization will be sceptical of the team's ability to lead them, and they will be sceptical about the restructuring.

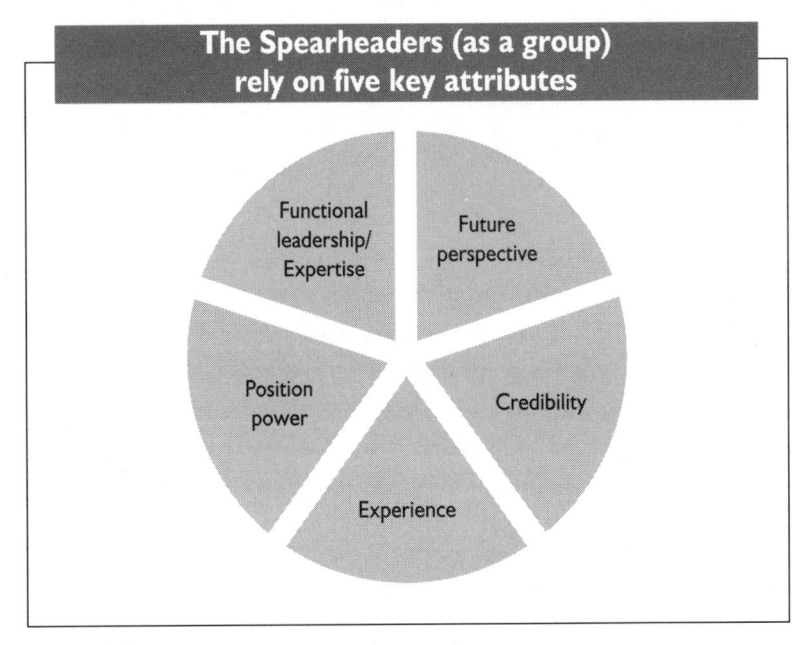

The Spearheaders (as a group) rely on five key attributes

- Functional leadership/Expertise
- Future perspective
- Position power
- Credibility
- Experience

Figure 3.2

As many members of the team as possible need to be people with good credibility throughout the organization. Accepted opinion leaders in the company who have earned respect through hard work, follow through on what they said they would do, and are equipped with social competence. These are the people who provoke the feeling, 'if he/she is part of the team, it must be OK.' They are likeable, capable and believable. And the more of these members you can pull together, the better. Those individuals are proven team players, and will therefore also be important in the functioning of the Spearheading team. So for reasons internal and external to the Spearheading team itself, you've got to find that incredible credible person.

The team also needs someone who's been around, who knows what's been done before and why things are done the way they are – someone who knows enough about the company's history and culture to help the Spearheaders understand what works well, what needs changing, and how that change can best be effected. The experienced Spearheader can be the guardian against change for change's sake, and the link between the past and the future. This individual is important to the rest of the company because the selection of someone with history in the company signals that tradition isn't being rejected outright.

Finally, the team needs a real forward-thinker. Someone with an eye to the future, and an ability to see how the company's future can unfold. It's important to be sure that the Spearheaders have that future orientation, and it's the future perspective person who will ensure that outlook gets its due share. One of the arguments made by those against getting involved in a restructuring is that it won't help the company in the long run anyway. It's the forward-thinker who will make believers of those who need convincing that the company will be in shape to face the future.

Choosing the right team of Spearheaders for a particular project is a delicate balancing act. Just as the company's leader is a role model, and his actions are a signal to the rest of the organization as to what is important or unimportant, the Spearheaders will also be viewed as a team of role models. The smooth-functioning consistency of the team, with its range of power bases covered, will show that top management is behind the plans it is promoting. A team with these characteristics, the desire to succeed, and the ability to work together can't be beat. If a team of Spearheaders without this chemistry is chosen, both the Spearheaders and the programme for which they were chosen are likely to fail. Top management should not underestimate the impact of this group, and should follow up regularly to see that the faith they have in the team is well-placed. If the group exists, but is not strong enough, all its efforts can be sabotaged, as the following situation illustrates.

> **Blocking restructuring**
>
> A European manufacturer of high technology equipment was planning a restructuring. The company's new CEO accepted a team of Spearheaders proposed by middle management to design and implement a supply chain integration project. The Spearheaders were selected from the functional groups that needed to co-operate in order to succeed in integrating the supply chain. But many of these groups were seeking to block the restructuring and protect their turf. They sent weak, ineffective candidates to join the Spearheaders. The Spearheaders' efforts were thwarted, and the project was unsuccessful: buy-in was never achieved. It looks as though this company will not survive the repercussions.

A pivotal task for the CEO is to choose and nurture the Spearheaders for each restructuring project. Since management's role increasingly incorporates both the day-to-day operations and restructuring, it is sensible to develop managers who can do both. Membership in the Spearheading Team provides valuable restructuring experience. Spearheaders learn how to achieve results within existing organizational constraints, and with limited formal authority. But the team should change periodically so that its members do not lose touch with the front lines and the company's regular business operations. This is especially important when it comes to developing strategy. The Spearheaders' involvement will make sure the strategy can be put into operation, and will make sure it is in touch with what can actually be achieved in the time available.

Becoming a Spearheader should be exciting, it should be a reward for successful work done well, and it should become part of the career path for promising individuals in the organization. Spearheaders will have to shoulder a heavy load, so it has to be worth their while. And senior management has to know whether they're doing a good job. That means rewards should match performance, and you should make a point of measuring that performance. Good performance is easy to describe: whatever it takes to effectively get the restructuring accomplished within a reasonable timeframe, with extra emphasis on the ability to get the changed organization working the way you want it to. It's more than just the restructuring that counts. You can *think* it's in place and working well, but the real test is in the staying power of the changes.

Challenge the enemies of a winning mindset

> 'People wanted to keep believing their old ideas about our market and customer positions.'

Being trapped in old ways of thinking can spell bad news in a quickly changing world. We're inundated: more demanding customers, deregulation, new markets, new competitors entering our markets, converging technologies and industries, exploding access to information. Old formulae will not succeed year after year, the way they have in the past. New, aggressive competitors will make it much more dangerous to rest on past victories. New markets will bring growth opportunities to those who can adapt. Converging technologies will quickly outdate conventional business practices. Alliances, mergers and joint ventures are increasingly popular as a way to globalize, and as companies merge with or acquire other entities, each will need to let go of some familiar cultures and procedures.

What frame of mind is most helpful to the entire restructuring process? What mindset do we need? How can we nurture an attitude, a way of looking at the company and the world in which it operates, that compels the company and its people to make the most of their opportunities? The enemies of a winning mindset are complacency and arrogance, narrow-mindedness and rigidity in thought and action, procrastination, fear and anxiety. Focus on their opposites as the keys to a winning mindset: characteristics and perspectives that will help a firm succeed in its restructuring. Even better, an organization whose people are always looking for a better way, who have a passion for new ideas, and who are proactive, flexible and courageous will benefit the company's day-to-day health, not just the issues related to restructuring.

Fight complacency and inertia

Complacency is the child of past triumphs, but also the forerunner of crisis. So often you hear of companies that have achieved tremendous success, only to rest on their laurels and be caught off guard by hungry competitors. The rose-tinted spectacles of success hide emerging threats, and everyone wants to believe that the good news will go on forever.

Complacency blinds companies to the need to restructure

'Difficulty getting all management to agree that restructuring was necessary.' — Manufacturer of investment goods

'Can't get commitment to the need for change.' — Telecom

'After the first restructuring, the company was financially OK again; it was then difficult to make clear that there was still a need for change, in order to remain in business in the longer term.' — Transportation

'The old home bases didn't want to accept the changed global business situation.' — Manufacturer of investment goods

'Some businesses and people believed that the threat would go away if they built a good story about why they didn't need to participate.' — Chemicals/Pharmaceutical

Once you're on top, you become everyone else's target. Competitors will be looking for ways to overcome the edge you've built, and the smart ones won't be doing so by imitation. Success can lull people into believing they make the rules. The German machinery industry is a classic example of complacency inevitably leading to crisis:

The German machinery industry

The German machinery industry dominated the world from the beginning of the Wirtschaftswunder (Economic Miracle) and up to the 1980s. They tailor-made machinery to exacting specifications, with uncompromising quality. They believed this customization and their unbeatable quality made them invincible, and so became distant and unresponsive to changing customer demands. The trade-off between quality/complexity and cost was tipping in cost's favour, but the German industry wouldn't see it. The Japanese stepped in to fill the void with more standardized products, and in the late 1980s the German machinery industry's share of the world market dropped significantly.

Inertia is a more subtle form of complacency. Theories of attribution tell us we believe success is due to our own efforts, while we usually try to make failure someone else's fault. So from the shop floor to top management, every success we have makes us more and more convinced that we're doing what is right. Academic researchers have found that companies can hold on to outdated assumptions for years, ignoring overpowering proof that the rules of the game have changed. As one restructurer put it, *'People believe in their old ways!'* We want to keep repeating the strategy that brought us success in the first place. That means a company that manages to shake out inertia has a tremendous advantage.

Think about inertia on a national level and most Europeans will squirm at least slightly. For example, the *Herald Tribune* reported:

> *'Where other countries have embraced global entrepreneurship ... France tends to see its economy and very identity threatened by innovations ... As Pierre Birnbaum, a political scientist put it, "Our problem is that we have not found the way to mod-*

ernize while preserving our imagined community." In other words, how do you leap into the world of the Internet and remain French?'[5]

And in a similar vein, *The Economist* lamented:

'For most of the past decade, Europe's history has been its biggest burden. In the second half of the 1980s, when America went through the most wrenching structural changes in 50 years, Europe tried to get away with doing nothing. Firms were holding on to old management hierarchies, ancient diversifications and outdated working practices, stuck in national markets and hemmed in by pervasive regulation. Europe seemed to be a fortress, designed not so much to keep out the Japanese and the Americans, but to keep out change ... The hardest part about giving up drink, they say, is admitting you are an alcoholic. This is what Europe has been doing in the past decade.'[6]

The solution to stamping out inertia and complacency? Create an edge in your company that always pushes everyone to do better. Refuse the *status quo*. Be proud of your success, learn from it, and start looking for the next one.

Royal Dutch/Shell

'In 1994, Royal Dutch/Shell made more than 7 billion ECU, up 33% from the previous year. But the committee of managing directors felt that the aggressive pace of change in the business world would overtake the company eventually, if they didn't act. They wanted to change before they had to ... [They saw] the need for breakthrough performance in an increasingly competitive world. They spelled out some specific threats in a series of workshops that were designed to shock, energize and mobilize the organization.'[7]

Shell says *'no'* to complacency. It recognizes that its successes won't live on perpetually. It uses success to build confidence in the ability to do better in the future, rather than as an excuse to do nothing. Shell recognizes that someone will always have a better idea, or will see a market in a new way, and that the willingness and ability to adapt quickly are critical.

Push out arrogance

Arrogance is the even more dangerous cousin of complacency. Complacency comes from the belief that you're successful, so you don't have to change. Arrogance is potentially more treacherous: belief that because you're the best, you can do anything *and* it will always turn out right. A complacent company is one that's caught napping, while arrogance spawns dramatic gestures that put the company at risk. The market leader in German premium pilsner converted its success to arrogance:

> **Brewery king**
>
> The company was so successful in the domestic market that it dictated market prices. Anything done by the company or its chairman was deemed newsworthy. The chairman started to believe he was invincible, and more than worthy of all the acclaim he received. He decorated the brewery in marble, and the walls of the headquarters with extensive and expensive modern art. But he didn't stop there. He believed he had the power to choose his market. He began drifting away from the core market that had always bought his product, and towards a more élite market, in the belief that the core market would never leave him. While he celebrated himself and his successes, his competitors were busily developing cheaper production methods and courting the market leader's alienated core market.

Arrogance led this company to abandon the principles that made it successful. That arrogance came with a price tag. The company's market share has tumbled from its once dominant position. The brewery king is not alone in his delusions of grandeur. Arrogance finds fertile ground in successful companies.

3 • A winning mindset

> **Daimler-Benz**
>
> Daimler-Benz has only recently recovered from Edzard Reuter's ill-fated goal of becoming the leading technology concern in the world. For a time he and his followers believed the company's success in automobiles meant it could be successful at anything it tried. Current CEO Jürgen Schrempp is taking the tough decisions needed to backtrack from that corporate arrogance and return the company to its original strengths. In just over a year the company chose to let the Dutch aircraft manufacturer, Fokker, go bankrupt; sold Dornier, another aircraft manufacturer; dismantled AEG, an electrical products subsidiary; and transferred its railroad traffic division into a joint venture with ABB.

A winning mindset has no room for arrogance. Leaders have to insist on looking at their companies and their strengths realistically, without overplaying past successes.

Unearth new potential

Breaking out of old thinking is not a luxury, it's a requirement. But it's harder to do than you might think. Over the last number of years most companies have developed some real skills in cost-cutting, and they're finding it tough not to use that recipe to solve every problem. Our research showed that 40% of companies seemed almost completely blind to issues beyond cost. And even those whose restructuring objectives related to better meeting customer requirements, and pursuing new market opportunities, turned to cost-cutting solutions and measured their restructuring success largely in terms of cost reduction and productivity improvement. Management recognizes that the challenges go far beyond cost alone, but to date has had difficulty in adapting restructuring activities to reflect that. Our view? In today's world you can never ignore cost, but limiting your thinking to cost alone will also limit your growth potential.

> **Breaking out of old thinking is not a luxury, it's a requirement.**

Three-quarters of the companies with top restructuring performance had changed ownership or management just prior to their restructuring. The implication: an injection of new blood was obviously necessary to get the company to challenge its thinking and to look outside its old patterns. Existing management is more often held ransom by vested interests and past decisions. That makes it difficult to see and support the breakthrough change needed to excel in the marketplace. Contrast the clean-slate, new-idea, absence-of-vested-interest manager with those described by less successful restructurers. In one company, *'The self-protecting attitude of senior management was the biggest obstacle faced in restructuring'*. In another it was the *'mental maps of the parent'*. The parent company saw one way of doing things and could see no further. In contrast, the top performers were able to achieve outstanding results, thanks in part to the open-mindedness of those at the helm.

Openness and responsiveness to new ideas is needed on all levels of the organization, but the signal for it really comes from the top. When we asked our restructuring Affinity Council how existing management could achieve the success that new management showed in our survey, an investment banker emphatically told us, 'Forget it. New management is the only way to get good new thinking.' And the stockmarket seems to agree. New CEO appointments usually trigger share price increases. That's what happened when Daimler-Benz was handed over to Jürgen Schrempp and when Peter Brabeck took charge at Nestlé.

The phenomenon isn't just a corporate one. Recent election results in the United Kingdom were accompanied by a boost in morale and in the stockmarkets. The long-standing Conservative government was short on new ideas, and the electorate and the markets showed readiness for a change.

If you're looking to keep your position, you as existing management really need to dig deep for the best ways to transform your company, unleash its potential and capitalize on emerging opportunities. Try inviting experts or peers for discussion rounds, visiting other companies' premises with open eyes, reading the business press and also listening to new hires in line management.

Open-mindedness is important on two dimensions, especially for top management (see Figure 3.3). CEOs need both the intellectual capacity to see the enormous breadth of issues they face, and the emotional open-mindedness that tells them cows shouldn't remain sacred for too long. There are many pressures bearing down at the same time, and the chances of successfully sleepwalking into the future by replicating the past are very slim. Instead, companies need to consciously anticipate pressures and how to respond to them. It is no longer simply cost or competitive pressure that push management, it's both pressures at once, along with a host of others.

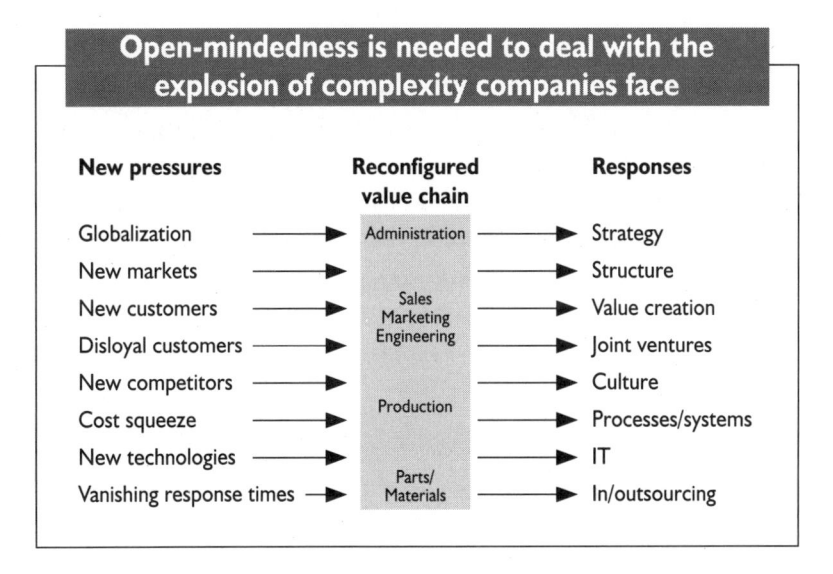

Open-mindedness is needed to deal with the explosion of complexity companies face

New pressures	Reconfigured value chain	Responses
Globalization	Administration	Strategy
New markets		Structure
New customers	Sales Marketing Engineering	Value creation
Disloyal customers		Joint ventures
New competitors		Culture
Cost squeeze	Production	Processes/systems
New technologies		IT
Vanishing response times	Parts/ Materials	In/outsourcing

Figure 3.3

As a leader you need to be the recipient of market and company signals. Strong leaders recognize that this is best accomplished with the help of the rest of the organization. An open and questing mindset within the organization will contribute to top management's understanding of pressures, threats and opportunities. As a corporate leader, you have to stretch to absorb more ideas and issues so that you can better guide and update your people. Stretch beyond existing patterns to search for the rich vein of gold – there aren't many places left where the gold nuggets are sitting on the surface.

For centuries, Europe's emphasis – manifested in its educational systems – has been on the intellectual, but in a way that encouraged narrow rather than broad thinking. Depth of expertise has been preferred to breadth, resulting in a narrow focus. Opportunities and threats that fall outside that focus risk going unnoticed. There seems to be a built-in bias in favour of the way things have always been done. European management needs to break out of that tradition, yet take advantage of the rich traditions of European industry as a foundation on which to build.

> *'Some see Europe's emphasis on "continuity" as a sign of strength. Pointing to the hollowing out of middle management in America, they argue that American firms rush from one management fad to the next. European companies, they argue, are more measured and less destructive ... The best European companies can combine the professionalism of American management, its discipline and flexibility, with a thoroughly European commitment to consensus and continuity. Europe's adaptation will be slow, and come in fits and starts. Yet as long as European companies are flexible and open to change, they will take strength from the past.'[8]*

So no European leader should try to get rid of tradition just for the sake of it. Nor should he blindly copy Asian or American ways in the pursuit of constant improvement. Instead, look at their strengths and see what you can adapt. When the Japanese started copying European high tech products, they left out the complexity that we in Europe see as essential to the customer. Our task in Europe now is to absorb Japan's aversion to complexity without compromising our unrivalled quality. This sounds familiar, but take a look around: not many European companies are working on it.

Anticipate needed change

You can wait for the problems to come to you, or you can address them before they arrive. Of course, a desperate situation makes it much easier to convince people of the need for action. A prosperous company may be too lethargic to make a choice; in a crisis, urgency is so great that no choice is left. Management may be more straightforward in a crisis situation, because everyone can see it's do or die, but without freedom of action it's 'stopping the bleeding' rather than opportunity creating. A frame of mind that looks ahead and strives to solve emerging problems rather than emergencies is the frame of mind that's needed when you expect change to be fast and furious, and when you expect competitors to be pulling out all the stops. No-one can afford to stand still for long these days. It's just a question of whether you look ahead and act ahead of crises, or let the problems find you.

British Airways

British Airways has adopted the pro-active approach. A difficult but tremendously successful restructuring in the 1980s turned the airline from one of the worst into one of the best, and Sir Colin Marshall, British Airways' chief, is determined to maintain that position. In the autumn of 1996 he announced another restructuring programme, aimed at fine-tuning the company's focus by outsourcing non-core business.

Airbus Industrie finds itself in a more delicate situation.

Airbus Industrie

The Boeing-MacDonnell Douglas merger makes it clear that Airbus is facing a difficult future. Airbus has the additional challenge of being run by people from a number of different cultures, each with a distinct view about what the company should or should not be. It will be interesting to see whether the company is able to mobilize and find a successful strategy for dealing with its strengthened competitor, or whether it will wait to react to what Boeing throws its way.

The bottom line: the sooner you recognize and act on the need for change, the better off you are. Anticipating – or creating – market shifts or competitive changes gives you more time to consider your options and plan responses. A restructuring based on clever anticipation of these external developments and on a realistic assessment of the capabilities hidden within the company is more likely to succeed than the nasty one done in reaction to a take-over threat or shareholder uproar.

Reactive restructuring means struggling for survival

'Restructuring was performed to save our relative market position.' — Automotive

'We restructured because we lost half our market share on our most important product.' — Manufacturer of investment goods

'Our restructuring was successful – the company survived!' — Chemical/Pharmaceutical

Pro-active restructuring means building for the future

'Developed better environment for the business to develop.' — Manufacturer of consumer goods

'Want to create a positive atmosphere where good ideas can grow.' — Utilities

'Just do it' — Chemical/Pharmaceutical

'Creating a sense of urgency' — Transportation

The whole organization needs to be on the lookout for new ideas and changing conditions. This means not only an open culture but also a climate of expectation. If people do not know you are waiting for their ideas, they will not tell what they have on their minds. You should set up an improvement programme, and give people a certain amount of time and resources to do their own research. 3M does this very successfully. Post-it came into the world this way. Europe needs to nurture similar success stories.

A winning mindset searches for the need to change, and seeks to change to avoid problems, but it doesn't champion change where none is needed. It's a delicate balancing act, and it's important to filter out the complacent voices when weighing the need for change.

Build companies poised for action

There's a need for organizations to become more flexible, adaptable, and reconfigurable, so that they are prepared to take on whatever challenges and changes they meet. That means the people that make up those organizations (at all levels), must also take on those characteristics. Gone are the days when employees simply repeated the same task over and over and over again, sometimes for their whole working lives. The rigid structures and rigid thinking that pervaded most companies until recently were entirely appropriate in environments where change was happening slowly. And just as success led to complacency, it has also often led to inflexibility.

Spearheading Growth

> ### Inflexibility
>
> During the course of a restructuring in a company located just north of Berlin, management realized that 122 of the company's welders would no longer be needed. By coincidence and good fortune, a factory in southern Berlin was expanding and needed 160 new welders. Arrangements were made to enable the north Berlin welders to transfer their positions to the factory in southern Berlin. Same pay. Same working conditions. The alternative was almost certain unemployment. How many welders took up the offer? Only two. The rest preferred unemployment to working in a new factory in new circumstances.

Now, with change accelerating, it's time to rely more on information, judgement, imagination, creativity and innovation. It's time to rely less on old structures, procedures, and safe havens. You and your employees need to be willing and able to adapt your work to changing circumstances. And with a flexible, open-minded approach, your employees can help you identify those changing circumstances. Rely on the front lines: they're closest to the market. Capitalize on what your sales people know and see rather than prescribing to them what they should know and see. Find out what people think rather than telling them what to think. That's a big change from 'the way things used to be.' It means new thinking, not only for the employees, but also for their superiors. Moving away from the 'command and control' mentality means that mistakes will occur, but a company that doesn't make those kinds of mistakes is probably not pushing hard enough to find its true potential. And a company that remains rigid and structure-driven risks an even graver fate – the inability to adapt.

> *Now, with change accelerating, it's time to rely more on information, judgement, imagination, creativity and innovation.*

Siemens

As Siemens grew over the years, it relied more and more on defined processes to control its operations. It became attached to the one right way of doing things – which made sense when it was growing steadily through the sale of mass-produced goods – and it devoted more and more people to making sure that those processes were followed. But that control orientation filled Siemens with many more people than it actually needed, and fostered a rigid mindset. The traditional approach made it difficult to keep up with speed-based changes that Japan introduced, and the company's cost base was much higher than its competitors. CEO Heinrich von Pierer took action against those traditions, insisting that the company benchmark itself against others, rather than continue to perpetuate its old ways. He also created independent business units, with the rights and responsibility to make their own profits. The company's growth and restructuring programme, TOP, compels each business unit to be responsible for its own growth and its own change in culture. And employees are now paid by results rather than by seniority. Siemens is learning that the legacy of past rigidity is an urgent challenge to overcome – it has already learned that it has no choice but to change repeatedly.

Cultural rigidity is an issue as well, as firms move to sell their products and services to new markets. The ever innovative IKEA learned some valuable lessons when it entered the North American market.

IKEA

'IKEA's entry into North America was supposed to be simple. It had already perfected its technique throughout much of Europe, and selected good US locations for its first stores. But the sales didn't follow. CEO Anders Moberg headed west to see what was going wrong. The European product lines weren't attractive to the US market, because people in the US just don't live the same way as people in Europe. The beds were too narrow, the glasses were too small (no room for ice), and the customers couldn't fit their sweaters into the shallow, narrow dresser drawers. IKEA, like Siemens, realised that its rigid way of looking at the world had to change. It adapted its product line for North America with great success.'[9]

Top management has sounded the siren. Across all industries they expect that with fast-moving markets and customers, restructuring will become continuous. But neither that message, nor its implications, have cascaded down through their organizations. Employees, because they've been through the pain of downsizing, still want to believe restructuring is a one time thing. They tend to believe it is only legitimate for a company in crisis. Employees identify **'the conflict of impressive profit increases versus continuing restructuring measures,'** and insist that there are **'too many restructuring programmes.'** That thinking must change. Restructuring is necessary to move companies forward – to deal with new challenges and create winning opportunities. It is no longer an emergency repair kit for companies in crisis. It is no longer a one-time cure-all. And it's not something to be dreaded – it's a way to get ahead. With everyone restructuring more frequently, competitors will be changing quickly and substantially, and you need to keep up. Everyone will have to accept the need to steadily improve the company and its prospects.

Learning contributes to the ability to be flexible. You'll be well served by people who are curious: those who believe they should never stop learning, and who are hungry to find out about new ways of doing things, new concepts, or broader job responsibilities. Learning about more than one job in the company makes them adaptable if and when job responsibilities need to change. A secretary who really listens and absorbs incoming messages could be a valuable contributor to customer service discussions. An accountant who wants to know what makes the customer want to buy the company's product, rather than just what the customer will pay for it, may figure out that the number of service calls is just as important an indicator of performance as the profit per unit. Learning about new technologies, new delivery systems, or new market areas will make it easier for your people, and hence your company, to adapt. And curiosity can generate ideas and concepts you may be able to apply in the business. People who want to learn and who insist on being flexible rather than clinging to old policies, hierarchies and procedures will be better contributors in the restructuring process as well as in day-to-day business.

Find the courage to make results-oriented decisions

Restructuring is hard work. So is adjusting to external, market-based thinking. And people, including outside stakeholders, will be sceptical. That is why creating and announcing a restructuring plan is insufficient. Restructuring is an active process that needs people (from all levels) who are willing to act and who do act. Many restructuring projects never get off the ground because people are reluctant to come to the end of their analysis – to take that first step towards action. The elusive perfect plan seems to be just around the corner, and they keep looking and refining and re-analyzing, without ever getting anywhere. Others take action, but believe any sort of action will solve the problems. Few take the tougher step of choosing impactful things to do. An action- and decision-oriented mindset is needed not only to carry out the restructuring, but to make sure the right restructuring gets carried out. The objective is not simply to take action, but to take meaningful action.

> **Lack of courage**
>
> The world's leading manufacturer of eyeglass frames built its reputation on fashion, which differentiated it from the other manufacturers who focused more on function. The company's original owner fell into the arrogance trap, and instead of concentrating on his business he focused on his private life. The company suffered, and was eventually sold. The new top man was more familiar with cost control than with the creativity on which this business thrived. His cautious nature led him to try to solve the company's woes through cost-cutting. It seemed like the safe, familiar route. What the company needed instead was a bold investment in design, to sustain the creative advantage that had made it a market leader. The focus on costs, and the lack of courage to invest in design, eventually stifled all growth, and the company never regained its former prominence.

Percy Barnevik, former CEO of the tremendously successful ABB, comments:

> *'You have to move boldly. You must avoid the 'investigation trap' – you can't postpone tough decisions by studying them to death. You can't permit a 'honeymoon' of small changes over a year or two. A long series of changes just prolongs the pain.'*[10]

Action-orientation is the final link needed to forge a strong restructuring mindset. The final piece to the mental quilt that will bring restructuring success.

Foster a winning mindset

'Inertia was our biggest obstacle'

All over Europe, people have come to realize: when things go wrong in a company or even an industry, it is often the mindset of the people involved that is the barrier to change. Many cases have shown that it is extremely demanding to induce change on all levels. But you can and you should, the sooner, the better.

Start now. Don't wait until you're face to face with an emergency restructuring. Build a positive, open, pro-active outlook throughout your organization, so that everyone is ready for change, or even better, so that everyone can help spot the need for change. The attitude or spirit in your company underlies the whole restructuring process. Be attuned to mindset before, throughout and after each of your restructuring efforts. Revisit it again and again – don't leave it to chance, because the spirit of your people drives everything that happens in the company.

The mindset you foster in your organization will contribute to the overhaul of national and European mindsets as well. The press regularly reports Europe's economic difficulties, attributing them largely to relentless regulation, inflexible labour forces, and governments' misplaced nationalism. But some countries are beginning to break that pattern. Notably, the Netherlands has navigated a path between left and right. Labour unions have accepted a degree of fiscal discipline, and as a result business has been willing to invest and create jobs. And the government has relaxed regulation, for example to allow for more part-time labour. Denmark, as well, has made it easier for companies to hire and fire, and therefore fostered job creation.

Countries are reflections of their people and their companies. There are signs that even in the countries more attached to the past, a positive, problem-solving mindset is beginning to have an impact. Philippe Jaffré of Elf Aquitaine has sparked other nationally owned companies to follow his lead, putting their top executives on the same footing as lower-level employees. And late in 1996, when Jacques Chirac was pressuring Air France to cancel its order with Boeing and support Airbus Industrie instead, CEO Christian Blanc insisted that the Boeing planes were important for competitive reasons, and if the government didn't like his decision, he would step down. His decision was accepted. The head of Usinor Sacilor, Europe's biggest steel-maker, which was privatized in 1996, notes:

'Politicians have learnt that the longer you try to win time, the worse it is. You cannot stop the world.'[11]

The forward-looking, customer-oriented mindset that is taking root in some of Europe's companies will also help reshape the political landscape and national psyches will again begin to believe that Europe can be a world power.

Where to start? The best place is top management. Top management involvement and commitment was the most important restructuring success criterion identified in the survey. If you, as top management, fail to broaden your outlook, it probably won't matter much to you whether the rest of the organization does. If your range of vision is narrow, and if you're reluctant to make bold new moves, chances are you wouldn't even notice the mindset in the rest of the organization. A winning mindset has to exist at the top if it's truly to catch fire throughout the firm.

There are different levels of engagement possible from everyone in the organization. Top management should be leading the way in open-mindedness, communication, high expectations and enthusiasm. When assessing the mindset in your organization, you have to think about what is fixed and what is changeable. Those

Spearheading Growth

that obstruct need to go, because they can impact the mindset of others in the organization, and they can damage your restructuring efforts.

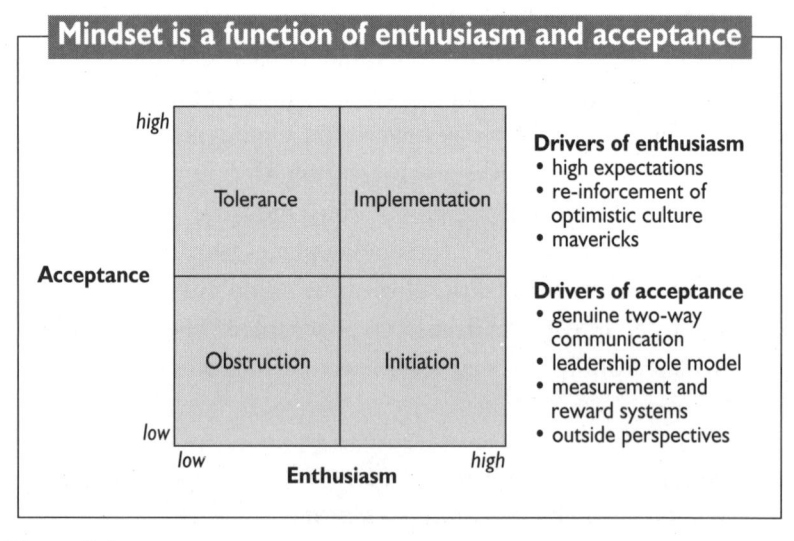

Mindset is a function of enthusiasm and acceptance

	Enthusiasm low	Enthusiasm high
Acceptance high	Tolerance	Implementation
Acceptance low	Obstruction	Initiation

Drivers of enthusiasm
- high expectations
- re-inforcement of optimistic culture
- mavericks

Drivers of acceptance
- genuine two-way communication
- leadership role model
- measurement and reward systems
- outside perspectives

Figure 3.4

Recognize, however, that someone you brand as a change resistor today, need not stay that way. Putting into practice the ideas we outline can turn someone who obstructs into someone who initiates or implements. There is no single key that will magically move one through this matrix. Rather, it's a combination of approaches, followed through consistently and diligently, that is likely to make a difference that counts.

How can you plant the seeds of a winning mindset, and what does it take to cultivate and renew them over time? There is an art to finding the drivers that will work for you. Start by identifying where you and your company sit in the matrix shown in Figure 3.4. Figure out whether acceptance or enthusiasm is lacking, or whether you need to boost them both. We've identified a number of ways in which you can disrupt a problematic mindset within your organization and replace

> A positive mindset supports your day-to-day operations as well as your restructuring efforts.

it with an enthusiastic and motivated one. Different measures will contribute to the development of different aspects of your mindset and that of your employees.

Mindset evolves gradually. There is no miracle cure for an ailing mindset. It took quite some time for most organizations to reach today's inflexibility and it will take time to dismantle. Don't wait. A positive mindset supports your day-to-day operations as well as your restructuring efforts, so the sooner the organization is energized, the sooner you will start collecting the benefits. Start laying the groundwork right away.

Search for new perspectives: learn what outsiders have to say

The belief that everything is OK can weigh a company down. There doesn't seem to be a reason for finding new ways of doing things, and even less reason to think about restructuring. It's human nature that we over-emphasize our successes and underestimate our weaknesses. But outsiders won't fall into that trap as easily. They see your company more objectively, and compare it to other companies they deal with. Not just competitors, but also those in completely different businesses. They can evaluate whether and in what ways you exceed or meet their expectations and where you fall short.

Pfleiderer

The CEO of Pfleiderer, a very successful wood products company, attributes part of his company's success to an insistence on listening to outsiders. Over the past years, the company has boasted double digit revenue increases, and has become the technology leader in four of its product lines. The CEO insists that he and his company regularly be challenged by outsiders, and credits those outside perspectives for getting the company to look beyond its traditional horizons and for getting the company to believe it can exceed its current performance.

The evidence in favour of outside input is strong. Not outside input to the exclusion of inside knowledge – that could prove dangerous. But nonetheless, there are clear advantages to looking beyond your own backyard, and to asking others what they see when they look in your backyard.

Philips

Companies like Philips, for example, try to get as much customer input as possible and try to turn even complaints into positive contacts. In this way, both Philips and its customers can develop new approaches and improve its customer/supplier relations.

We were very surprised, therefore, by the opinions of those in the restructuring Affinity Council about how best to fight complacency. Less than 30% pointed to external input as a primary way to kick-start new thinking. Performance measurement and target setting play important re-inforcing roles in developing the company's mindset, but where will those targets come from? If they're imposed from the top, you're likely to get compliance, but not commitment. Employees will work towards your targets because it affects their pay cheques, but they're less likely to be unearthing new directions themselves. The mindset goal is not obedience, it's contribution, and by exposing everyone in your organization to new ideas and perspectives, you'll unlock their thinking and benefit from their creativity.

These challenges can be addressed in three ways: by adding managers and experts from the competition, by benchmarking or through discussion with other companies that are in some respects comparable. This is easier said than done. The new people you recruit from outside will be very unpopular with their new ideas, so they have to be supported by top management without being given too much special status. And top management also has to make it clear that it is not just criticism it is looking for but constructive and even hands-on input. This input is best given and exploited in the context of internal projects that may even have a motivating influence on those old hands on the team who used to see things one way only.

If you'd rather not recruit external knowledge and judgement, there are plenty of other sources of outside information – suppliers, creditors, even board members who have experience with other companies. And there's nothing like an angry customer to get the point across about what you're doing wrong. The benefits of outside input are twofold: the evaluation of your enterprise, and the chance to learn about what is going on outside your company. Because it's easier, companies tend to focus internally, but beyond cost savings, it's tough to achieve real breakthroughs without understanding what's going on outside.

Encourage direct contact with all kinds of external sources throughout all levels of the organization. Even an offhand remark or a conversation that takes an unexpected turn may uncover opportunities. What do others see about your business, your market, and your competitors that is passing you by? For example, your company probably has standard approaches for evaluating competitors and market opportunities. Hearing how someone else goes about those things can open some valuable doors. The sources of information they use, their interpretation of market circumstances, each of these new perspectives gives the company a new slant when looking at its own position.

Benchmarking is a good form of exposure to outsiders. It's a way of learning about new ideas, and it's attention directing. If a company has superior performance to yours, that doesn't mean you have to imitate exactly what they're doing, but it does point to where improvement is possible. And benchmarking can go beyond those in the same industry – looking at how similar processes function in other industries can also be the source of inspiration.

Exposure to outside perspectives will help achieve:

- an objective view of performance – attacking complacency and showing that there is room for improvement
- an objective view of others in the market – again showing where there is opportunity for improvement
- a new way of looking at the facts – those with experience in different industries may provide a whole new outlook. Within our own areas, we're always at risk of seeing the trees but not the forest. An outsider can pull us out of that habit.

Metallgesellschaft

In the case of Metallgesellschaft, the call for an outsider became stronger after the company had suffered an economic breakdown. The new perspectives offered by Kajo Neukirchen had already been the key to survival for Klöckner Humboldt Deutz, and the former Hoesch AG, where he launched life-saving restructurings. His success continued at Metallgesellschaft. The former managements in all these firms did not foresee problems and couldn't find a way out on their own. In each case the outsider carved a path back to success.

But outsider input on its own is not sufficient to implant the new mindset, as the following situation at a steel mill engineering company demonstrates:

3 • A winning mindset

Complacency

The owner of one of Europe's leaders in steel mill engineering worldwide saw tough times ahead for his company if it did not change. Profits were deteriorating, and he foresaw a drop in demand as the steel industry suffered. Riding the wave of 30 consecutive years of profit, his executive team did not see any need for action. Complacency ruled. The owner brought in outside consultants to provide an objective assessment, to identify where processes could improve and to find ways of improving market performance. The outsiders were able to persuade top management to make some changes – costs went down, sales processes improved, skills were upgraded and a specific expertise was identified and supported. However these changes coincided with a short-term market improvement, so the executive team decided that enough had been done, and that any potential problems were cured. They slid right back into the complacency they had suffered from earlier.

In this situation the outsider information was forced on the restructuring participants, and they accepted it to the least extent possible – they *tolerated* the restructuring, but nothing more. They didn't obstruct and they didn't abdicate, but they didn't really change their fundamental beliefs either. That's the difference between compliance and commitment: doing something because you have to but not because you're a believer. Believers are a sign that the winning mindset has really taken root.

Communicate, and communicate again

Communication at all levels and in all directions is vital. You probably have not yet achieved mind-reader status. It's through dialogue that you refine and test ideas. It's through communication and conversation that you get across what's important and not important. That holds for your company as well. Your chances of getting something done, and done right, increase substantially when you actually communicate what you are trying to achieve and why. Why did the top executives at the steel mill engineering company stop short of achieving all they could with their restructuring? They never *really* believed in or understood the need for change. They hadn't *really* understood that market orientation was critical to their long-term survival. Time spent explaining and proving that the need for change was real could have turned them into supporters. Contrast the steel mill engineering company with a recent privatization project in Southern Europe:

> **Privatization project**
>
> This was the first experience this manufacturing company or its employees had had with restructuring. Recognizing the importance of getting the buy-in of the group, the restructuring team set up a big meeting involving all employees. The meeting described the reason for the restructuring, the way the process would work, and what employees at all levels could expect. There was unlimited time for discussion and questions. All of the employees' concerns about the process and how it worked received answers. The meeting was a terrific success. It resulted in such overwhelming buy-in that the project finished ahead of schedule.

There are a few lessons here. First, the communication was direct and unlimited. Second, the communication style suited its target audience. Not every culture would find that forum appropriate. It's important to try to think like the people with whom you're communicating. In some situations it may make more sense to have smaller meetings, or to build up to meetings after other communication efforts. Third, the meeting – real two-way communication – allowed people to ask questions and to be convinced. If you are certain that your plan is in the best interest of your company, you should be able to convince your people. Mere distribution of information doesn't allow for this all-important dialogue. A sceptic who reads what you publish has a good chance of remaining a sceptic. A sceptic who gets a chance to question you and let you prove your points is much more likely to be convinced. And you may score another benefit of two-way communication: some of the sceptic's questions may point out issues or considerations you hadn't thought of – ones for which it's worth changing your plans.

Members of our restructuring Affinity Council agreed on the importance of communication. We asked them how best to improve employee involvement and commitment to restructuring, and their overwhelming first choice was open, honest communication. Once again we'd like to challenge their thinking. The Affinity Council members focused on the general communication *statement*, to the virtual exclusion of specific actions that would result in that very communication – such as soliciting alternatives that meet the restructuring objectives. Saying involvement and communication are important is easy. Living those statements takes effort and commitment. But that effort will pay off through your employees' valuable contributions to your restructuring.

We make a big deal about communication and employee commitment because we suspect many managers will insist they've heard it all before. That may be so, but it's our *recent* survey that tells us these issues are still rampant. And quotes from our survey hinted that top management sometimes resents the time and work involved in securing a winning mindset (see below).

Do leaders really believe in the need for communication?

'Communication inside and outside the company was very difficult.'
Chemical/Pharmaceutical concern

'Explaining, communicating, and gaining commitment was a big obstacle because it requires a lot of effort and energy.'
Financial services

'Time and cost for communication with all employees was an obstacle in our restructuring.'
Transportation company

'The most difficult thing we had to deal with was explaining the reasoning behind the chosen restructuring.'
Manufacturer of investment goods

It seems top management would really prefer to deal with facts and figures rather than people. Does that describe you?

Lots of information – communicated readily, clearly and without reservation – helps build the trust that will persuade people to work with you and towards the company's vision. A shortage of information usually generates anxiety that works against creating the mindset you want and probably wreaks havoc on productivity and customer service as well. The crisis that everyone sees but no-one talks about is much more ominous than one that's openly discussed – implications are explained and solutions can begin to be developed.

Why has tradition, especially in Europe, dictated that employees have limited access to information? In some situations, especially with mergers and take-overs, there are legal restrictions, relating to issues such as insider trading, that prohibit companies from publicizing information until certain agreements have been finalized. Beyond those legal restrictions, there has been a strong school of thought that information shouldn't be disseminated throughout the organization, but should be guarded jealously, or it could fall into the wrong hands. Nonsense. If you know something, tell it. The information will eventually come out anyway – why not let it out sooner so people have time to adapt and to add their feedback? Percy Barnevik agrees:

> *'You don't inform, you over-inform. That means breaking taboos. There is a strong tendency among European managers to be selective about sharing information. We faced a huge communications challenge right after the merger ... Just days after the birth of ABB, we had a management meeting in Cannes with the top 300 people in the company. At that meeting, we presented ... the essential principles by which we run the company ... I told this group of 300 that they had to reach 30,000 ABB people around the world within 60 days – and that didn't mean just sending out a document. It meant translating it into the local languages, sitting with people for a full day and hashing it out. Real communication takes time, and top managers must be willing to make the investment.'*[12]

Old thinking held that information was power – and to a great extent that still holds true today. In many companies it's guarded by those who get it because that gives them a status higher than those who aren't in the know. A company that wants to profit from people involvement, however, has to find other ways of satisfying those status needs, or find ways of eliminating them. Information and communication will help people to do better work.

Finally there's the possibility that senior management doesn't want to tell what it knows because it doesn't want to be on the hot seat. Senior management may have to justify its past actions and may face criticism on its planned actions. Horror of horrors – communication with your own workforce could actually force you to disrupt your own mindset! It could actually give you exactly what you want: employees who take an interest in the company as a whole, not just their own pay cheques.

> **Try to understand how your people are thinking and then figure out what you need to communicate to meet their needs.**

Communicate in a context that's accessible for employees. Don't just talk strategy, talk strategy and back it up with your best understanding of what that means for the way people have to do their work. Try to understand how your people are thinking and then figure out what you need to communicate to meet their needs. One of the important questions they'll be asking – maybe not out loud – is 'what's in it for me?' That's something your communication has to address – not just what you want to accomplish, but why your people *should* want to help you out. Think about the language you use in your communication. Phrases like 'work smarter' are tempting, but think of your employees' perspective. These phrases imply everything they were doing before was wrong. That's not the right message. You want them to understand that things have changed and what worked before doesn't work now. More complicated to explain, not as catchy on posters, but much more satisfying to the receivers of the information.

We can't stress strongly enough that when you think you've communicated fully and clearly and when you think you've got all the feedback you could ever hope or expect to get, *do it all again*! Time after time we come across situations where top management believes it has communicated extensively, only to find out that employees see the situation quite differently.

And it's important to check whether your message is getting through.

> **Feedback**
>
> When two complementary professional service firms merged, the change team took extra care to concentrate on clear and extensive communication. At various points through the process they asked for feedback on how they were doing. Employee ratings were consistent: they felt the change team wasn't communicating enough and they didn't feel they knew enough about what was going on.

There are two further considerations when you're evaluating the effectiveness of your communication. Don't just measure whether the message was received, see if it's resulting in the changes you hoped for. If the message is getting through, but nothing's changing, that can be as serious a problem as not getting the message through at all. And follow through on the *two-way* promise. Many companies set up hot-lines for their employees to express concerns or ask questions, for example. But they either never get as far as listening to those calls, or never communicate back to the employees. There's a feeling that communication has fallen into a black hole. Boasting of two-way communication, but not following through, can frustrate employees and turn them into non-believers.

Take communication all the way to transparency. Let everyone see decisions and results, so that peer pressure can work its magic. Those that are members of a group are expected to act in the interest of that group. If some project or some person is getting an unjustifiable share of resources, and the group sees it, there will be pressure to put a stop to it.

Keep performance expectations high and reward achievements

Companies can extract extraordinary achievement by setting expectations so high that 'business as usual' can't meet them. Show the depth of your belief in your business and your people through your confidence in their ability to do better. Don't simply set outrageous goals – your expectations have to be credible. Carefully think about what would be possible with some real initiative. Make the goals consistent with the company's vision. If you just say all performance results have to increase by 'x'%, it will be taken for what it is, management hot air. Find the dimensions that really could improve dramatically with extra effort and ingenuity, and focus your high expectations there.

That's Part 1: you back up your conviction that the company can do better by setting very high standards for achievement. Part 2 is measurement. Measure yourself and your workforce against specific goals. And be open-minded about the measures you choose – don't cling to the narrow financial measures that most companies are unable to shed.

This talk of measurement is too obvious? Think again. Our research found yet another paradox – a discrepancy between what management says and what it does. No matter what respondents said they were trying to achieve, when asked how they were measuring success, the focus was overwhelmingly on *cost* (see Figure 3.5). If the bottom line is all that counts, there are all kinds of short-term ways to manipulate results to show good short-term performance, often at the expense of the innovative and forward thinking outlook you want to encourage.

We asked our restructuring Affinity Council about the reason for this cost obsession, and the most prevalent answer was that cost measures were easy to understand. That reflects the complacency and inertia that we're trying to stamp out. Relying on cost measures simply for convenience implies that you don't really care about the new vision and strategy that you've been promoting. Cost as a primary, or as the only, performance measure only makes sense when cost leadership is your strategy. But even then, the

Customer-focused restructurers rely on cost measures

Top restructuring objectives and triggers

- New market opportunity
- Change in customer requirements
- Significant improvement in market position
- Significant increase in customer focus

Top performance measures

- Cost
- Number of employees
- Productivity

Mismatch!

Reflects triggers, objectives and performance measures of 40% of the sample whose restructuring was motivated by customer/market concerns

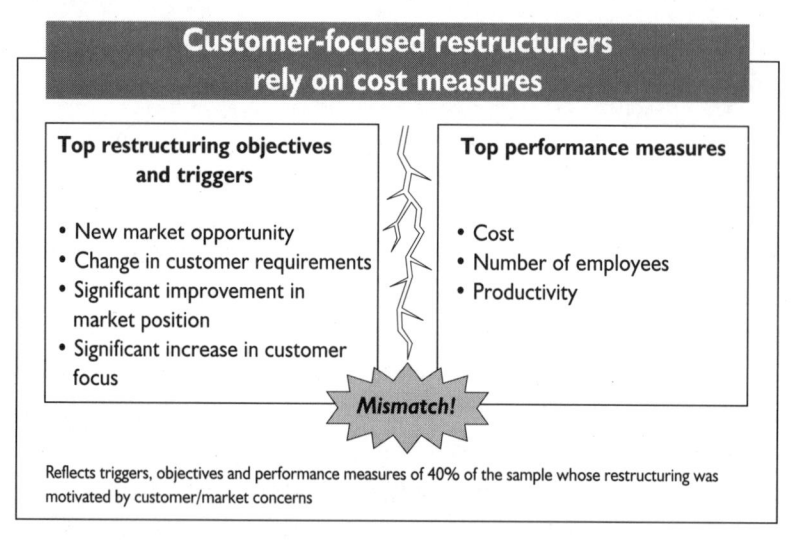

Figure 3.5

measures need to be expanded beyond your company's borders. If the goal is cost leadership, measuring your own skill at cost reduction only tells half the story – you also have to compare yourself to your competitors. If you want to see results, and if you want your people to focus on more than cost reduction, you need to take the time to design performance measures that work. The right measurement system can encourage a broader perspective. Furthermore, as we'll detail later, it can help keep your restructuring on track. A well-designed performance measurement system focuses on the results that drive performance.

One approach that many companies have found helpful is the *Balanced Scorecard*. The balanced scorecard directs attention at a number of issues. Rather than focus on one key measure, it looks to see how the company is doing from a customer's perspective, from the shareholders' perspective, from an internal operations perspective and from an innovation and learning perspective. It demands broader thinking and acting, because it measures more than one dimension of a company's performance.

The concern that Affinity Council members expressed about measures being well understood, however, is relevant. Very elaborate and complicated measurement systems and reports risk being poorly understood and rarely used. Simplicity is important. Figure out what measures will encourage the kind of actions you believe will deliver results. Performance measures drive activity. People will work to achieve what they are being measured upon more diligently than they will work to meet vague goals.

Take advantage of the measurement system's ability to direct attention. It will guide people towards appropriate activity. We looked at Hoechst, the chemical/pharmaceutical company, to learn how measurement helped guide its successful restructuring.

Hoechst

Hoechst had evolved as many German companies did after the Second World War – in an environment where growth just happened, and where it made sense to reward people on the basis of output, not profitability. In the 1980s and early 1990s, however, serious industry overcapacity meant that encouraging output through performance measures no longer made sense. Jürgen Dormann, chairman since 1994, signalled the changing of the guard. The company decentralized, giving business units much greater autonomy. Greater responsibility accompanied that autonomy. Each business unit had to meet a certain level of profitability within three years or close down. So far so good for this new take on performance measurement. In 1995 Hoechst reached its best profit level in ten years and in 1996 had a profit of 1.4 bn ECU, a further 24% increase.

The measurement system is a good way of keeping up the pressure, but it needs to be flexible enough to give people the freedom to figure out their own solutions. It directs attention, but doesn't tell them exactly what to do. At Hoechst, the general direction was set, but the business units have the freedom to figure out how to get there. Precisely because performance measures are such strong attention directors, however, those designing the measures have to pay careful attention. In addition to keeping it simple, make sure you think carefully about what you are motivating people to do, to prevent situations such as this one at a large consumer goods company.

> **Share options**
>
> In an effort to align the interests of owners and other stakeholders, the company motivated corporate managers with generous share options. Managers became so intent on the short-term share price that they mortgaged sources of supply and distribution channels. This alienated employees and suppliers, and made it hard for the company to satisfy its customers profitably. Competitors moved in and took significant market share.

Nurture an expectation of change

Top management seems to understand that change is inevitable and change will be frequent. That message needs to reach the rest of the firm as well. Expectations have to be managed. Convey your conviction that restructuring will be around for a while, and that stable, certain situations are very unlikely to characterize the future. Part of the difficulty in getting people on board for a restructuring comes from their belief that restructuring is a one-time event reserved for crisis situations. One restructurer noted that employees identify the *'conflict of impressive profit increases versus continuing restructuring measures.'* It's better to be told: 'we're not sure what the future will hold, but these are the principles we plan to follow in addressing the issues we face, and as we learn more we will tell you', than to be told nothing and read about the announced restructuring in the local press.

The reactions of middle managers to restructuring and downsizing in 'dynamic' companies and 'troubled' companies supports this notion. Research finds that the middle managers that had the least resistance and worked most productively were those who understood that the implicit contract of bygone days, where middle management was equivalent to job security, was no more. Their companies – the dynamic ones – fostered independence rather than obedience. These managers accepted that their tenure with the company depended on a match of skills to needs, and that for both the manager and the company this was unlikely to be lifelong. They didn't expect, as did middle managers in troubled companies, that things would eventually settle down. Armed with that perspective, these managers made sure their knowledge and training was up to standard, to help them in their current and future positions. They built their own security. The managers in troubled companies, who didn't want to admit that the old days were gone, more closely tied their own fortunes to those of their companies. The middle managers in companies who performed best after downsizing, demonstrated a much better understanding of their company's strategy and direction than those in companies who weren't performing as well.[13] The managers who adapted had a better understanding of where the company was going and how they fit, but they did not have certainty.

Make room for mavericks

A company that's filled with people who all think the same way risks the corporate inertia and inflexibility that many restructurers complained of. Living with mavericks and tolerating failure can generate *within* your organization the broad perspective you'll also be seeking from outside. Mavericks can help *you* broaden *your* perspective. Realize that not all the bright ideas have to come from you or others in top management. Capitalize on the inspirations that would never come to light if you didn't permit anyone to rock the boat. If you never make any mistakes, you're missing opportunities. And if you want people who are innovative and open and willing to consider all possibilities, you've got to expect some mistakes.

> ### Richard Branson
>
> Richard Branson is a maverick. He dares to be different. He does not focus. His companies, ranging from air travel to pop music, achieved success by flouting convention. Branson cultivates his maverick image, and even this attracts customers. He explains: *'I like taking big risks, I like to do things differently and to make them better'*.

While encouraging mavericks, at the same time you want to protect against a crippling mistake. How? Find ways to test ideas. Don't say 'no, that's too risky'. That would discourage the innovators and send the message throughout the organization that you aren't interested in taking risks and trying new ideas. Instead, try 'that idea could have merit – now figure out a way that we can test it cheaply, and we'll go forward'.

A tolerance level for mavericks, and for the occasional mistake, is important for fostering the pro-active, forward-thinking action-oriented attitudes that you want to cultivate in your firm. If failure is outlawed, people will believe that it's safer to do nothing and to try nothing. That doesn't work in a rapidly changing world. But it also doesn't mean anything goes. Everyone has to understand that this is no *carte blanche* for making mistake after mistake. We're talking about a willingness to try new ideas. That sometimes means taking action without 100% certainty, but there's no need to leap into risky ventures with very low levels of certainty. It always makes sense to mitigate risks, but sometimes you've really got to experiment to score big breakthroughs.

Help the culture evolve

Culture evolves from a set of values – and the set of values that gets the most air time is that held by top management. Culture drives the informal processes of the company – and often those informal processes are the real cogs that turn the wheels of the company. Culture is the foundation for the way in which the people in the company work, interact, and behave. It's critical to shape the culture in a way that strengthens the can-do/will-do/want-to-do mentality of the organization. And it's incredibly hard to change. The more history there is, the deeper the culture goes. That may be one reason that Europe's attempts at becoming more flexible and adaptable and customer-oriented are experiencing such hiccups, while North America's upheavals occur more readily. Europe has a longer history and its culture is more ingrained. Even as Europe moves to privatize its industries, governments try to protect monopolies and national heroes – they seek to preserve old cultures rather than to evolve new ones. Privatization's intent is to create more dynamic profitable companies, but State intervention persists.

> It's critical to shape the culture in a way that strengthens the can-do/will-do/want-to-do mentality of the organization.

Simplicity is important when the environment is complex. Adding complex, dynamic internal principles to an already complex external environment would be overwhelming. Simple principles give people guidance, but don't tell them exactly how to work or what to do. People can develop their own self confidence and independence within the company's general rules. And as we saw earlier, those who are independent and self-confident within a general framework usually develop more flexibility and resourcefulness. When they achieve something, there's a real sense of accomplishment, because they figured it out themselves. See what's happened at Oticon, the Danish hearing aid manufacturer.

Oticon

'Oticon's share of the world hearing aid market dropped 50% during some intensely competitive years in the 1980s, when Oticon was slow to incorporate technological breakthroughs – such as the hearing aid moving from behind the ear into the ear. The company started cost-cutting, but realised that cutting costs alone would never get it back to its Number 1 world position. Instead, it aimed for a fundamental change in culture – one which encouraged team work, flexibility and adaptability. These characteristics would give Oticon the new ideas and creativity it needed to build on its niche strategy of differentiation from its large, diversified competitors. In 1991, Oticon chose to lay the groundwork for the new culture in the struc-

> ture and systems of the organization. It eliminated all offices, and virtually all paperwork. No more status symbols, titles or job descriptions. They were replaced by people with multiple skills and talents. There were no jobs – everyone was expected to create new ones. The thinking was that this new anti-structure would encourage people to form appropriate teams as needed, and to address the problems that they felt were important. The driving force would be the project, rather than the people managing it. The new culture was built within a supportive and appropriate environment and Oticon's profits have been on the rise ever since.'[14]

Deliberately acknowledge what your culture is trying to achieve. If the company is embarking on a series of projects that will create a world of discomfort, say so. And make an important hallmark of your new culture, the willingness and ability to adapt as the company needs to. But in doing so, respect the culture you're leaving behind. You want to move people towards a new, more appropriate culture for the times. Because culture is such a foundation of who people are and how they relate to the companies for whom they work, it takes time to change. It builds from many small steps. *You*, yourself will find it hard to change, and you should be the easiest sell of all.

Culture is difficult to change because it is invisible. You really have to search out situations where the old culture continues to take precedence over the new. Think about how much of the old culture you have to change, and how much you can keep. And keep paying attention. Your company is more likely to slide back into its old culture than magically embrace the new one, so care must be taken to re-inforce new cultural values constantly. At Oticon, the transformation was accompanied by lots of press coverage and publicity, which made turning back to the good old days a virtual impossibility.

Don't try to change the culture without people noticing. Draw attention to what you're leaving behind and why – so that there's real understanding about the new culture and why it's important. And don't forget that, especially when it comes to culture, the leadership provides the ultimate role model. Create and reward some heroes who have successfully adapted the new culture and benefited the company. Those examples show the rest what it is that the company is looking for. Results – a tangible demonstration of what can be accomplished with the new culture – are the most powerful persuaders. And sometimes it means bringing in some new people who aren't so attached to the old culture and the old way of doing things. British Airways is widely acknowledged to have engineered a miraculous turnaround – and culture was at its root.

British Airways

In 1981 British Airways lost almost 1 billion ECU. BA meant Bloody Awful as far as the passengers were concerned. Within five years, the company was boasting the highest profits in the industry, and almost all employees bought stock when the company went public in 1987. British Airways' cultural shift began when top management decided the company was in the service business, not the transportation business. The entire workforce started down the new road by attending two-day culture change programmes. Managers went through a five-day version of the same programme. The new training was consistent and thorough throughout the organization, and it benefited from extraordinary top management commitment. Top management lived the programme, and were visible supporters of the changes. Compensation schemes were adapted to the new focus as well, with up to 20% based on management's success at adopting the service orientation. And the company's Marketplace Performance Unit had as its mandate the task of objectively looking at the airline's performance through its customers' eyes. Everything the company did was working towards the common goal of making travel with British Airways an unbeatable experience.

There's an additional twist to culture in our increasingly global world. Despite the disappearing borders and corporate boundaries, different companies and different countries or regions still have very different cultures. So not only will companies face the challenge of adapting their cultures to be more pro-active and open to change, they'll have to address differences across national and regional cultures. The best weapon in this regard is awareness

– from both sides. It's a case of knowing that the way you act may be perceived differently when you're not in your home country, and being ready for that difference. In the Netherlands, for example, it is much more acceptable to be open with your criticism than it is next door in Belgium.

The power of those cultural differences is striking. Look for truly pan-European companies – beyond ABB and Guinness/Grand Metropolitan, now Diageo, there isn't much to talk about. Shell and Unilever have straddled the Dutch/Anglo cultural differences successfully. Airbus is working on it, but they've had some real struggles addressing the different philosophical and economic viewpoints of the partner companies/countries. Europe has been working at breaking down barriers and unifying its market for some 40 years, but the struggle is not over yet. And it's an important struggle, for the easiest markets to succeed in are usually the ones closest to home.

A company's culture underpins all of its activities. The right culture and value system supports all of the characteristics of the restructuring mindset that we have been talking about. The culture you want to evolve in your company is one that supports the winning mindset that's important to restructuring in a rapidly changing world.

IN BRIEF

Mindset

- Psychological barriers impede European companies' success: complacency, arrogance, narrow-mindedness, rigidity, cowardice and procrastination are the enemies.

- Leaders alone cannot change a company.

- Spearheaders leverage strong leadership and act as role models during the change process.

- A winning mindset is generated not only by benchmarking, open and honest communication, high expectations and empowerment, but also by a culture that makes room for mavericks and mistakes.

4

Strategy demystified

Focusing on essentials
- Start with a vision
- Set the strategy
- Go for growth
- Aim for relevance

'Definition of a mission – clear objectives and convincing strategy – was the key to our restructuring'

4 • Strategy demystified

Strategy development has a reputation for being difficult and complicated – the secret and perplexing domain of a few key people at the top because no one else is capable of understanding. Management literature devotes volumes to the mysteries and intricacies and problems of strategy. Management fads look for new ways to describe strategy and magic formulae for foolproof strategy development. Or, strategy development has a reputation for being shallow and meaningless – an annual ritual which goes through the motions of getting some kind of plan down on paper, and adds up departmental plans to come up with corporate strategy, rarely fighting conventional wisdom. We challenge both those perceptions. Instead, look at strategy very simply: what can our company do to secure its market in a way that's difficult for competitors to imitate? What do our current and potential customers want and need, and how can we deliver it in a way that helps us achieve competitive dominance?

> **A truly effective strategy grows from creativity, thought and deep understanding of the market and its future directions.**

Our conviction that strategy development need not be mysterious doesn't mean that strategy is obvious. A truly effective strategy grows from creativity, thought and deep understanding of the market and its future directions. It develops from foresight and a willingness to look over horizons. And our conviction that strategy development need not be mysterious doesn't mean that it need not take place at all. Running a business without strategy is perplexing at best, and at its worst, disastrous.

> ### Cost-cutting
> A national railway system is in desperate need of restructuring and has responded by launching a cost-cutting programme: costs must drop as quickly as possible to eliminate the annual operating losses of 430 million ECU.

'Sounds good,' you say. 'Cost-cutting is often unavoidable.' That's true, but there's a problem. How can management even know whether cost-cutting is best if they don't know where they want to take the railway? And picture cutting costs in that vacuum. Is it important to keep all train routes, or can the less travelled, unprofitable ones be eliminated? If some routes can go, the railway can concentrate cost reductions on closing railway stations, stopping repairs to obsolete lines and simplifying scheduling. Will it be important to keep the existing equipment indefinitely? If so, an across-the-board cut in costs, including preventive maintenance and repair, could spell disaster. And that across-the-board cut is the likely reaction when strategy is sidelined. Without a vision, and without a strategy that explains how to reach that vision, cost-cutting could leave the railway worse off than before it started.

Cost-cutting and downsizing *are* sometimes necessary, but they should form part of a coherent strategy, not be an end in themselves. Let's look at a company in a similar situation that took a very different approach.

> ### A growing company
> An automotive parts manufacturer with over 20 billion ECU in assets was incurring dramatic losses, and would not survive without significant and immediate restructuring. The company decided to exit ten of the 14 businesses it was in, retaining only those that were actually creating value, had technological and/or cost advantages, and fitted strategically with the rest of the portfolio as well as with current and future markets. They reviewed the 20 plants they were keeping, over a 12-week period, and identified over 3 billion ECU of improvement potential which they implemented immediately. The result: by dropping 30% of its assets and growing the remainder by 50%, the company is larger than when it started.

This company developed a strategy, and resisted the temptation to blindly cut costs in response to a sea of red ink. The result? A growing company. An across-the-board cut in costs – the non-strategic solution – would have left weak divisions even weaker and made strong divisions vulnerable.

Strategy provides guidelines for everyone to follow, to figure out what they will do and what they will not do. It gives us the context we need in order to sort out the many decisions we face.

Why do we emphasize strategy so strongly in a book on restructuring? Restructuring is the repositioning, resource alignment, and cultural and organizational change that results in a reorientation of value-creating mechanisms and enables the company to achieve its strategy. Restructuring starts by figuring out what the company should look like to get where it wants to go and what it has to do to get there *fast*. European executives agree that restructuring will be necessary as never before in the coming years. With change happening more frequently, no strategy will remain relevant for long. The re-alignment of strategy to vision will need to happen more frequently, and restructuring will surely follow.

In our experience many companies don't recognize the connection between strategy and restructuring, often because their view of restructuring is narrow. To them it is a response to a crisis, with little strategic thought, or a patchwork solution to a series of problems. More often reactive – emergency – in nature rather than pro-active – elective. Think about it. In pro-active restructuring you choose when and how to change, while in an emergency those choices disappear. Which would you prefer?

We look at a continuum of company circumstances from stable prosperity at one end to crisis at the other (see Figure 4.1). The greater the crisis or urgency, the less freedom there is to act. Restructuring in an emergency almost always means struggling for survival or buying time for the more fundamental restructuring that will inevitably follow. In contrast, those who prosper maximise their degrees of freedom and have full potential to uncover the strategies that will turn them into leaders. Make the search for room to manoeuvre constant, otherwise competitive pressures will propel your firm towards the prison of crisis.

Spearheading Growth

Strive to move from emergency to elective restructuring

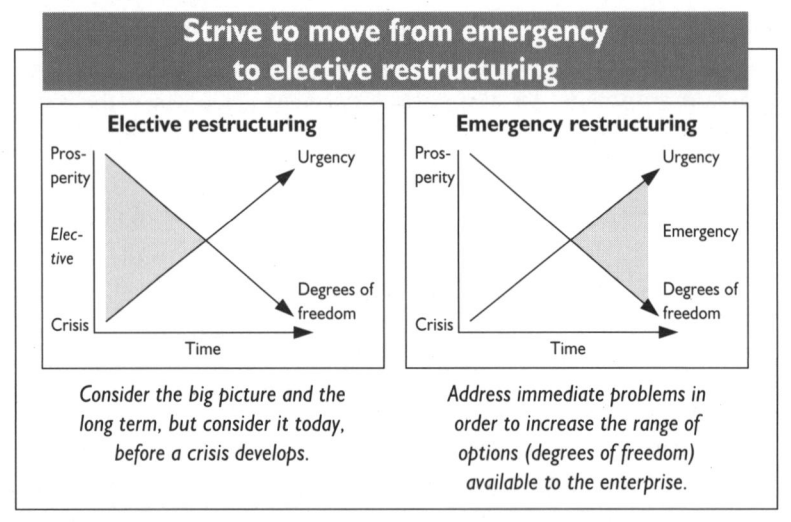

Elective restructuring	Emergency restructuring
Prosperity / Elective / Crisis vs Urgency / Degrees of freedom over Time	Prosperity / Emergency / Crisis vs Urgency / Degrees of freedom over Time
Consider the big picture and the long term, but consider it today, before a crisis develops.	Address immediate problems in order to increase the range of options (degrees of freedom) available to the enterprise.

Figure 4.1

Recognize where you are on the continuum. It sets the context for your strategy and your restructuring needs.

Crisis

When a computer hardware manufacturer entered the crisis segment of its continuum a few years ago, the priorities were to cut costs, reduce the scale of operations, and focus on the core business. Instead, it began to explore options, develop marketing strategies and reassess its business.

Under no immediate pressure

At the same time, a major oil company at the other end of the continuum, although under no immediate pressure, embarked on a programme of cost-cutting, downsizing and refocusing.

By failing to match their agenda to their prospects, both companies destroyed value. Preoccupied by its time-consuming analysis of strategic options, the computer firm's condition went from critical to terminal, ending in bankruptcy and a fire sale to competition. Focused on short-term issues, and full of political infighting over threatened job cuts, the oil company failed to explore new opportunities to create value, and thus put its future stability in jeopardy.

The oil company's mistake was not that it tried to fix things that were not broken, but that it failed to match its solutions to its problems. It was right to restructure, but wrong to restructure as if there was a crisis; it chose the wrong kind of restructuring. Elective restructuring is all about making choices. Emergency restructuring is all about surviving and getting into a position where there are choices to make.

It's time to make restructuring pro-active. In a crisis, there is little room for creativity to act, little ability to act strategically, and little chance of leaping ahead of the pack. Moving restructuring ahead in the typical corporate cycle may just help ensure the cycle's troughs aren't as deep. Make restructuring a way to ensure you meet your strategy, not a reaction to a failed strategic effort.

Start with a vision

'The starting point for breakthrough restructuring was a clear focus on future direction'

If you cannot take the time to teach a group of people how to build a ship, then implant a longing for the broad sea – that's how Antoine de Saint-Exupéry put it. What he wanted to get across was that without a vision any effort will be meaningless and also resultless.

So top management has to answer some basic questions before the strategy topic is tackled. Where do you want to take your company? What do you want to be known for? What do you want to achieve? What are the underlying principles that guide your organization? A corporate vision answers all these questions. It's the end goal strategy is trying to meet, and it's the underlying foundation for restructuring, but a well-conceived vision can do much more.

Let's face it. Nearly everyone has been through tough times at work lately. Most of your employees will have lived through at least one downsizing somewhere, may face a growing workload, and certainly feel less job security than they used to. So why would they co-operate in another restructuring? They need a reason, and a strong vision can be that reason. Restructuring has damaged company loyalty, and employees are learning to look out for themselves first. To change that, the starting point is vision.

Vision is a picture of where the company is heading, communicated on a level beyond mere facts and figures. It has an emotional appeal – it's something to believe in. In the best of all worlds, vision helps match the company to its employees: only the believers will stay. If the vision doesn't strike some kind of emotional, inner chord, then it will be difficult to get more than a superficial commitment to working towards it.

Vision signals that the company knows where it is going (see Figure 4.2). Shared vision generates or justifies pride in the company, and confidence in its future. It's a reason to go through all the hard work that will be necessary to achieve that future success. Think again about the people running the railway system, in the Case Study at the beginning of the chapter. They know they're in for a terrible time. More work, lots of problems, an uncertain future. But they don't know where any of it is leading. They don't know if the extra effort will be worthwhile. A vision could be the light at the end of the tunnel.

4 • Strategy demystified

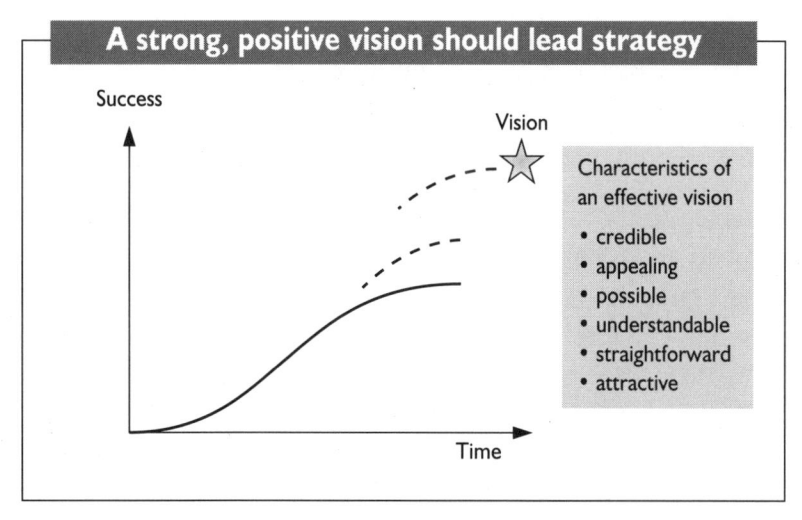

A strong, positive vision should lead strategy

Characteristics of an effective vision
- credible
- appealing
- possible
- understandable
- straightforward
- attractive

Figure 4.2

In today's Europe, where structures and safety nets of the past are being torn away, and the future holds more uncertainty than present generations have ever seen, vision becomes even more effective, and has even more power to give your company an advantage over a competitor who hasn't been able to capture the hearts and minds of its employees.

The good, the bad and the ugly

If you're a sceptic about the importance of vision, you've probably seen too many mediocre, poorly articulated, or meaningless visions. A good vision takes serious effort. You'll know you've got it right when:

- it provides strategic direction
- it captures the imagination
- it is specific enough to be believable

Spearheading Growth

- it is realistic enough to be achievable – though not without serious effort, tenacity and ingenuity
- it is appealing on an emotional level
- it is a source of pride: something you want to say out loud.

Why are there so many bad visions out there? Where are we likely to go wrong? The fact that most companies now *have* visions means most top managements believe creating a vision is a good idea. Let's look at some different visions and identify some of the traits that make the difference between strong, effective visions and those that don't make the grade (see Figure 4.3).

How do you rate these corporate visions?

	Good?	Bad?	Ugly?
Manufacturer with an impeccable technical reputation seeking to keep its competitive advantage: *Innovation has tradition*			
Airline: *Become the world's favourite airline*			
Financial institution focused on commercial lending: *We'll find a way*			
Consumer goods packaging company: *Number 1 in the world in our segment of the industry*			
Transport company: *15% return on assets*			
Steel industry: *Steel technology for strong ideas*			
Construction company: *From a master builder to a system integrator*			
Electronics manufacturer: *Let's make things better!*			
Large pharmaceutical producer: *New skills in the science of life*			

Figure 4.3

The best visions generate both strong internal direction and excellent messages to communicate to existing and potential customers. They make it clear to those inside and outside the company where priorities lie.

British Airways

British Airways' vision was outstanding in that dimension. Every employee and every prospective customer knew where the company wanted to go: 'Become the world's favourite airline' is simple yet meaningful. BA correctly understood that improved service would lead to more sales and would ultimately result in higher returns – the transport company's vision. The difference between the two? BA explained the vision in an appealing way, and in a way in which its employees could take pride. The transport company offered no emotion, only dry statistics; no hint of how to achieve its goal or of what kind of company it wanted to be.

Then there's the consumer goods packager (see Figure 4.3). Its vision is too vague. It's a vision that every company would like to claim, but very few would have a realistic hope of achieving. It is so ambitious, it seems unrealistic. And it's short on content: how exactly does the company see itself becoming Number 1? What does 'Number 1' mean? Revenue? Volume? Kilos? Profit? What industry segment? What does 'the world' mean? All the continents? The EU? The Western Hemisphere? What will be the differentiating characteristics that make it happen? There's nothing to grab hold of here for employees; nothing to capture the imagination. A vision needs to be aspirational, not generic.

> The best visions generate both strong internal direction and excellent messages to communicate to existing and potential customers.

It's important not to let the marketing prospects of the vision statement overwhelm its purpose in defining where the company is headed. The example from the steel industry sounds impressive, but does it help at all in understanding what the company wants to achieve? Not really. Something about technology, but whose strong ideas? Their customers? Their own? Will employees be able to grasp where the company is headed? Not likely. The need for a vision statement is primarily internal and it should not be replaced by a fancy marketing statement that doesn't get the internal job done.

Creating a vision is worth the time it takes. It's the starting point for getting the buy-in of major stakeholders. If the vision is not credible, there's sure to be trouble ahead. It's the starting point for your strategy – the target you're aiming at – and as such it underlies your restructuring as well. But this is a road that goes in both directions. You need a vision to provide a target for strategy, but just as importantly, your vision loses credibility if you do not support it with your company's actions.

Building a compelling vision

Vision will only work if it only appeals to the people in the company. It's not as simple as applying another company's successful vision. It has to work in your company.

It's not easy. Don't expect to wake up in the morning, magically knowing what your company's vision should be. If you do, congratulations! But for most of us an effective vision is the result of serious groundwork. The final product – the concise phrase that triggers clear and desirable images, and provides a target for the company's strategy – is the refinement of a core picture of the company's future which grows from lots of digging and thinking and foresight and imagination.

The work of developing a vision is an opportunity in itself for building the corporation's culture and for reinforcing its forward-looking spirit. The vision will be stronger if a group develops it. You want to be sure to involve the best brains in the company, and some key outsiders, if they can kickstart thinking in new directions. Solicit ideas from different levels in the corporation. Look inside and outside the company and think about what different forms the future could take. Analyze the industry, know the market as it is today and imagine how it could evolve. Judge how you can push forward that evolution. And look to other industries for a fresh view. Test whether the breakthrough moves in other industries have applicability to you.

It's important to get some distance from the day-to-day, to unleash creativity and uncover potential that's not inhibited or coloured only by today's pressing issues. Start with limit-free thinking. Assume anything is possible so that you see the whole range of possibilities. Then move in on what's most attractive and most compelling for your business. This is where the open-mindedness and broadness of mindset we insist on for restructuring first starts to pay its dividends.

Developing a vision is a process that *should* take time. A vision should have a certain degree of staying power, so look around, get ideas from both conventional and radical sources, and really think through the implications of the options you are considering. Reap the benefits of the enthusiastic, innovative outlook that you are nurturing.

It's important that those within the company take responsibility for developing the vision. This isn't an activity that should be outsourced, as it often is, to a favourite advertising agency. An advertising agency can be the key to helping your company communicate its vision, but the vision needs a solid understanding of your company's strengths and future opportunities, and the place to find that is within the company itself.

Set the strategy

> 'Our restructuring gave us a much clearer company profile, and as a result we have grown and improved profitability'

Armed with a clear view of the company's vision and potential, it's time to choose the strategy that your company should follow to achieve those aims. Be careful not to complicate the strategy development process – just at the point when it's important to be clear and straightforward. But also make sure you've gone far enough. Have you really developed a strategy, or is your plan something less? Think about what strategy means: a way of doing things, and a choice of what to do, that will captivate your customers and frustrate your competitors.

In the rapidly changing environment to which we're all trying to adapt, it's important to remember that strategy is not forever. It's the way you want to make your move, given the current situation, and in full knowledge of the fact that circumstances will likely change. But once again, we warn against change for change's sake. It's critical to re-examine your environment, and the appropriateness of your strategy regularly, not so that you can change, but so that you can gauge whether you *need* to change.

While the nuances captured in a strategy seem endless, it's liberating to realize that there are only two major strategies to consider: differentiating yourself from your competitors by finding a unique way to focus what you offer to your customers, or becoming a cost leader in your industry.

In most industries there's a continued downward pressure on costs. Relief from that pressure comes to those who are able to offer a package of benefits which customers agree is unique and therefore worth paying something extra for.

Consider the computer industry. Companies introduce new innovations at high prices, retain that benefit for some time and then eventually come under pressure from competitors to lower prices. That's been the case for hand-held calculators, for colour monitors, for laptops. Each innovation eases the price pressure, but usually not for the long term. The same is true of many other products, for example, many white goods. Our interpretation of this phenomenon has two key implications: those who excel in their industries are those who are able to differentiate themselves from their competitors and thus benefit from more room on price, or those who are able to make cost reduction breakthroughs. The two strategies of focused differentiation or cost leadership. Even for those who do not choose a strategy of cost leadership, it is critical to have an eye to costs, in anticipation of the eventual pressure that will come to bear from that side.

The most important thing about strategy, no matter which one you choose, is that it has to matter to your customers. If your customers or potential customers won't care about the changes you're making, then they're probably not very strategic. Here's how one restructurer described it: *'Satisfying our customers is and will be the major challenge. Our ability to cope with and master this challenge will secure or jeopardize our future success.'* Keep the customer front and centre. It is a simple, foolproof way to make sure you're really talking about strategy and not just tinkering with existing operations.

Beware of impostors

It's easy to lull yourself into being satisfied with something less than strategy. To form a strategy takes time and reflection, two precious commodities when you're already operating full steam on your day-to-day business. But take some of your precious time to review and renew your strategy – to test its relevance against what you know about the world. Chances are your strategy will need regular revision and will lead you to repeated restructuring.

There are those that argue that all strategy is emergent – that you don't really know what your strategy is until after you've implemented it. The difficulty with that view is that it leaves you short on guiding principles. Each decision you make has to be made from scratch. A true strategy provides a context within which to evaluate actions and opportunities.

In our experience, there's no way out: the best performances come from those who take strategy seriously and don't settle for something which falls short. Let's look at the impostors, and why you can't count on them to make the grade and ensure your continued competitiveness.

Doing what you've always done

Strategy needs to evolve as circumstances do. The pace of change in markets, in deregulation, in competitors, and in technology means that the strategy that you devised some years ago probably doesn't make sense any more. Looking in the rear-view mirror is a good idea when you want to go in reverse, but it's a dangerous approach when you want to move ahead. If you don't regularly revisit your strategy, you're probably making a mistake by calling it a 'strategy'. More likely it's a guarantee that you'll fall behind your competitors. And one of the consequences of falling behind is that you are more likely to have to restructure with your back to the wall. Your choices become limited, and you give up, at least in the short term, the opportunity to bring full creative thought to the strategy for making your company excel.

> ### The Swiss watch industry
>
> The Swiss watch industry is a classic example of an industry that looked backwards rather than forwards. In the early 1980s, the industry was at death's door. It plummeted from being the world leader to having only 2% of worldwide sales. Swiss watchmakers, despite having perfected the quartz movement, remained craft-oriented. They were more interested in defending the art of watch-making as they knew it than they were in exploiting new technology to make cheaper and more accurate watches. Their insistence on doing what they had always done came at tremendous cost, and virtually handed the market to the Japanese, for a while.

The average manufacturer in the Swiss watch industry, in doing what he had always done, didn't evolve with changing times and customer tastes – until Nicholas Hayek came along with the innovative Swatch and changed the rules of the game once again.

Benchmarking

Benchmarking is an important tool, but it doesn't replace strategy. If one of your competitors has a big lead on you in some important competitive dimension, the sooner you know about it the better. When you meet, or even exceed those benchmarks, however, you will only have succeeded at following someone else's strategy. You'll be at the mercy of your competitors' strategies. Worse yet, you may end up following part of Company A's strategy, part of Company B's and so on. Fragments of strategy that may not fit together at all. The best you can hope for is that you'll keep up with the rest of your industry. You'll never achieve a real breakthrough, and you'll usually be playing catch-up. The short-term advantage of introducing a new procedure or tactic will always go to the other guy.

Business process re-engineering

Business process re-engineering, the re-organization of a company into processes and a new look at how to carry out those processes, does lots of good for lots of companies. It points out inefficiencies in processes, and it prompts companies to think about new ways of doing things. Its focus on process thinking is typically a better link to what the customer needs than the traditional functional routes were. But business process re-engineering isn't strategy, and it's dangerous to get the two confused. Re-engineering, by its nature, doesn't look at the company as a whole. It looks at and improves pieces of the company, but not the whole business. It can delude you into thinking that you've solved all your problems, when in fact you could be completely on the wrong track when it comes to the big picture. A Northern European shipbuilder makes the risks of re-engineering to the exclusion of strategy painfully clear.

> **Northern European shipbuilder**
>
> This major shipyard went into business process re-engineering with a vengeance, and it reaped all the benefits you could expect: accelerated, more efficient processes, culture change from rigid to open-minded, cost reductions. But there was one big problem. While the company focused on itself and how it could improve, the market changed dramatically. The newly re-engineered company found that it had become expert at building products that no one wanted any more. The company nearly re-engineered itself to death. If not for some niche products and services, the shipyard would not be around today.

Cost-cutting

Our opening examples make it clear that cost-cutting is only a pale imitation of strategy. The benefits of cost-cutting can enhance a targeted strategy. However, if the sole objective is to reduce costs, without an understanding of where the company wants to go *after* the cuts, vulnerability and the need to cut again are the likely outcomes. A number of studies confirm that downsizing or cost-cutting in a strategic vacuum is dangerous. The likely result is not achieving the savings you hoped for, falling behind your competitors, and having to cut again. A 1994 survey found that two-thirds of the firms that cut jobs do so again in the following year.[15] And another survey of 1005 down-sized firms found that only 46% had realized lower costs and only 32% had increased their profits.[16] Here's what happened to a European conglomerate:

> **European conglomerate**
>
> The conglomerate faced eroding profits, and chose cost-cutting as its response. All 14 of its businesses were told to cut costs in order to improve the company's position. This effort wasn't very successful, so more cost-cutting followed – a spiral that continued, with the businesses getting progressively weaker, until the firm's eventual demise. A post-mortem showed that most divisions were too small ever to compete economically in their sectors, but a few had strong promise. Had the conglomerate looked at its situation strategically first, it could have sold the businesses with no stand-alone potential, and used the resources to build up the promising divisions.

Budgeting

Budgeting is sometimes equated with strategy development. By getting each department to justify all its activities, senior management hopes to be able to aggregate these plans into a strategy. But budgeting is a way of operating, not a way of generating strategy. It's breaking the strategy into pieces and seeing what it means for everyone. Strategy should synthesize, not break into parts. And budgeting is inherently short-term. A budget reflects a specific time period, say the upcoming year, and beyond that you're facing a blank wall. Strategy should be more forward-looking.

Taking on the whole world

This impostor describes the company that doesn't want to miss any opportunity, so follows up on all of them. One problem: not all opportunities are good ones. Another problem: if someone's looking for an expert, this company's name will likely never come up. And it isn't a strategy, because it doesn't lead to a differentiated competitive position. When resources are scarce, this approach gives no guidance as to where to invest them, since in the absence of strategy, everything seems to be important. Strategy not only helps you know what you will do, but also what you will *not do*.

> Strategy not only helps you know what you will do, but also what you will *not* do.

In our experience, many companies accept one of the impostors as a replacement for true strategy. Or they fall into their strategies by default, or settle for something that is too vague to be truly helpful. Very few companies hold out for the real thing. Those few companies that dare to really articulate a strategy reap significant benefits. Without question, they achieve superior results; they lead the pack. Top performing companies point to well-conceived strategies as a key to their success.

Restructuring success builds on strong strategy

Reasons given for restructuring success:

'Restructuring based on sound strategy'

'We reviewed the principal threats and opportunities for each of our key business units and from that reaffirmed our strategy'

Enough about what strategy isn't. Let's turn to the two basic strategies: focused differentiation and cost leadership. Think about the last round of strategies you considered. Every one of them, provided it was a real strategy and not an impostor, focused on something either that would set you apart from your competitors or intended to turn you into a cost leader. The first strategic choice, therefore, is whether focus/differentiation or cost leadership should be your approach. Assess how much leverage each of these strategies will bring you relative to your competitors, and where you feel your particular strengths and opportunities lie. We look at each of these strategies in detail, so that you can think about what's most appropriate for you.

Focus: the courage to choose

The strategy of focus capitalizes on your company's unique strength – or identifies a unique strength that your company should develop. It is a self-reinforcing strategy. By choosing a particular dimension on which to compete, you can focus attention on what it takes to excel in that dimension. As a result of that focus, expertise grows, and your company becomes even more able to excel. The focus lies wherever you believe you have or could develop an unrivalled strength that would be attractive to your customers and prospective customers. It could be a certain customer segment; it could be a certain package of benefits; it could be a particular geography.

A manager whose company struggled through a painful restructuring commented that *'unclear priorities made our restructuring difficult'*, while a successful restructurer told us his *'restructuring was a success because we achieved focus on core business and less dilution of key resources.'* That's the reason focus is so important. It means you make the best use you can of your limited resources. This thinking was confirmed by participants in our Restructuring Affinity Council.

When we asked them how best to achieve focus, the Number 1 answer was always, 'Concentrate resources and strengthen competencies.' Resources are rarely limitless, and a strategy which strives for differentiated focus helps companies to choose where to put their energies. Here's a company who learned the hard way about the cost of an unfocused business approach.

Unfocused business approach

A significant player in the European floor covering business was competing in 12 segments of its industry, and was proud of its hundreds of product lines. Careful analysis showed that in every segment in which they did not have a critical mass compared to the industry, they were making losses. Those losses were putting such a strain on resources that the company was unable to acquire companies with good potential to bolster its position in segments where it was strong. In contrast, the competitors in the industry with clear focus were the strongest and most profitable players in the industry.

In the floor-covering company's case, the inability to focus on profitable lines of business led to a host of missed opportunities and below-par financial performance. In contrast, Winterhalter Gastronom looked for a way to build on what it was good at. It used focus to achieve world market share leadership in a segment of the commercial dishwasher market. Manfred Bobeck, a director at Winterhalter, tells the story:

> ### Winterhalter Gastronom
>
> '"We analyzed the total market for commercial dishwashers and found that our world market share was about 2%. We were an also-ran. This led us to totally redirect our strategy. We began to focus solely on hotels and restaurants; we even renamed our company [adding Gastronom]. We now define our business as supplier of clean glasses and dishes for hotels and restaurants and take full responsibility. We include water-conditioning devices and our own brand of detergent in our product line. We offer excellent service around the clock. Our world market share in the hotel/restaurant segment is now 15 to 20% and climbing. Nobody can match us any longer. It's easier for us to adjust our systems to the needs of hotels in different countries because they are similar everywhere. It would be difficult, however, to adapt our systems to the needs of different customer groups because those are very different. Hotels in Asia and Germany are more similar than hospitals and hotels in Germany. It's that simple!" Small, even tiny, niche markets can become amazingly large when extended to the whole world.'[17]

Winterhalter focused on one industry segment, and that focus enabled them to develop a product offering and expertise that was matchless in their industry. They were disciplined in their approach to the market – refining and improving their product, and leveraging that expertise to give them a global reach. They didn't let themselves get distracted, and they didn't dilute their efforts.

A company that has made tough choices, that knows what business it wants and what it doesn't want, can have real advantages over a company with scattered interests. The focused company can more quickly determine what information and trends are relevant to its business because it is clear what that business is. It saves time and resources because the whole market-watch activity is more efficient, but more significantly, it can beat a less focused company in response time.

Deutsche Bahn AG

Deutsche Bahn AG (DB AG) is working its way through major transformation by focusing on what it needs most to stay in business: the customer. Quite a change for the former East and West German railway systems which in the past as State-owned 'enterprises' lived by rigid rules and regulations that rarely considered the customer. But DB AG's recent initiatives show a real recognition that unless it provides a service the customer wants, it won't stay in business. These initiatives include improving comfort and speed in long-distance passenger traffic, providing travel information by telephone, reducing waiting times when buying tickets, and better security at the stations. The importance of the customer has found its way into performance appraisal as well. Performance is now largely evaluated by measuring improvements in customer satisfaction. Employees' taking responsibility is encouraged, especially if it leads to happier customers. DB AG knows the road will be long and difficult, but it has made strides by, first, identifying the importance of the customer and second, reflecting that focus in both its action plans and its performance appraisal systems.

Why do some companies discount the importance of focus? What's the real difference between the top performers and the rest? It's the courage it takes to choose a specific path. Many of us are reluctant to close off options, just in case there's an opportunity in one of those options one day. But that's not strategy – that's just keeping busy. Strategy means choosing. Choosing what you will do and what you will not do. If you really want your company to make its mark, you have to *choose* in which area that mark will be made. Daimler-Benz is a good example of both a company that lost focus, and a leader with the strength to re-take that focus.

Spearheading Growth

Daimler-Benz

The company built an impeccable reputation as a luxury automaker after the Second World War. In the 1980s, however, it began a series of acquisitions into unrelated fields with the objective of becoming a 'technology concern'. It was no longer clear what business Daimler-Benz was in, nor where it should concentrate its efforts. Its financial performance suffered seriously as a result. Not only was the company not creating value, it was busily destroying it. Daimler-Benz' current CEO, Jürgen Schrempp, moved quickly to get rid of a number of shaky subsidiaries. The company has returned to its traditional focus, and is delivering improved results.

The participants in the Affinity Council confirmed that focus suffers because people are unwilling to choose (see Figure 4.4). The greatest impediment to strategy development, in their view, was the absence of strong leaders willing to make choices. The Affinity Council members have identified the problem, but each of them will have to take a deep breath to make sure they go beyond the words and follow up with action. The second most prevalent response, short-term results orientation, also shows a lack of courage. Management opts for the easy way out – a short-term fix – rather than identifying a strategy and undertaking a restructuring to build for the longer term. It's the cowardly mindset we identified earlier – the one that Percy Barnevik emphatically believes will hurt more in the long run.

Development of a strategy for restructuring is impeded by

- 15% The feeling that the company needs to do everything at once in order to survive
- 4% Using benchmarking as a substitute
- 49% Absence of strong leaders willing to make choices
- 32% Short-term results orientation

Source: Restructuring Affinity Council

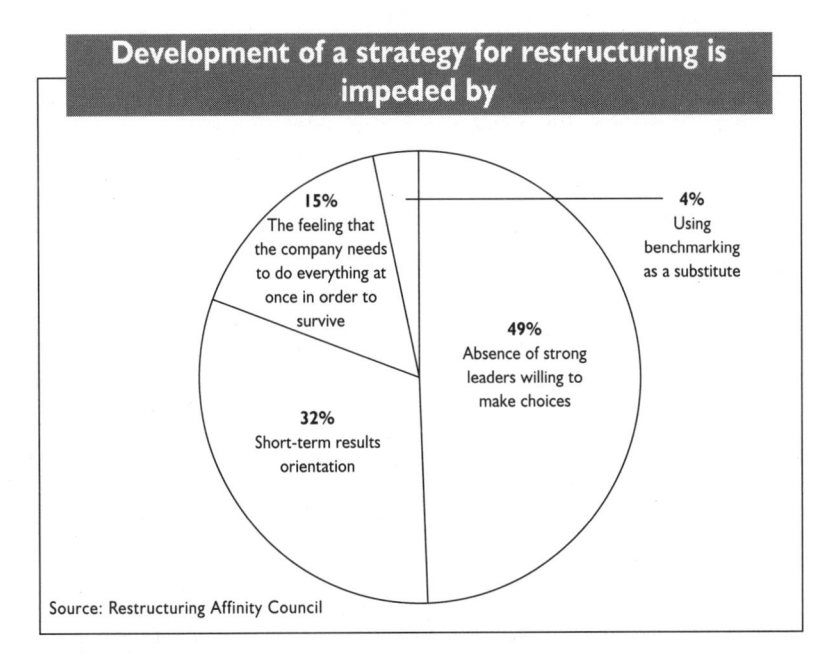

Figure 4.4

Customer orientation needs to be coupled with an understanding of your competitors – current and future, so that you can spot value migration early. Value migration means a change in where the value is generated. In the computer hardware industry, for example, the value has moved from the actual computer to the spare parts and hardware enhancements that are needed immediately after the initial purchase.

Everyone should be watching to see where the value is moving, but it's especially critical if you've adopted a strategy of focus: you want to know well in advance if the value is migrating away from your business and towards a different one. The sooner you know, the sooner you can adapt. That's one of the reasons it's so important to be open-minded and look ahead. The best of all worlds, better even than spotting value migration trends, is to create and initiate those trends. If you anticipate not only where the industry is going, but your customers' future needs, you can ensure that value migrates to your offerings.

A company that's clear about its business is most likely better at it. Focus fosters expertise. Nokia went through the pain of having scattered interests, but has emerged as a company with excellent focus:

Nokia

Nokia started out over 100 years ago as a small pulp mill in the village of Nokia in Finland. Over the years, the company expanded into a wide range of industries including rubber, chemicals, flooring, ventilation systems, and eventually telephones. When the company experienced declining sales in the 1980s, the CEO went on an acquisition binge – buying up companies that looked like they could compensate for the drop in sales in its existing businesses. This led them to enter the colour television and computer businesses, but in virtually all of its segments Nokia was too small to be a truly global player, and the company's fortunes continued to fall.

When a new CEO took over in 1992, he used his new broom to sweep clean, exiting unprofitable businesses and putting money and people into the mobile phone and telecommunications businesses. The direction from top management had finally become clear, and everyone in the company understood what the company was trying to achieve. He reinforced the entrepreneurial culture he felt would lead to differentiation in the telecoms and cell phone industries. He hired new managers who had studied outside Finland and brought international perspectives with them. The size of Finland's own market is so small that the company had to include international markets in its efforts: the strategy was to get global leverage of the company's outstanding competencies in cellular phones.[18]

The contrast between the two CEOs is striking. One grasped here, there and everywhere – a classic case of thinking you have to do everything in order to succeed. In contrast, the current CEO, Jorma Ollila, looked at the potential of Nokia's many product lines and businesses, and decided to concentrate resources and expertise in a growth market where the company had strong competencies.

One of the arguments against focus, usually promoted by those unwilling to make tough choices, is that there's too much risk in putting all your eggs in one basket. That perspective assumes that you choose your focus and stick to it blindly. Clearly a dangerous idea. Instead, if you choose a strategy of differentiated focus you'll need to pay particular attention to the environment; to developments in your industry and to your customers. It's crucial to recognize early when there are changes pending that will impact your chosen focus, so you can adapt. It helps if the focus is a customer need rather than a particular product. If you concentrate on meeting that need, your products will evolve as the customer's circumstances do. If you focus on a particular product, you risk the fate of the shipbuilding company we described earlier: being saddled with a perfect product that nobody wants.

Focus nurtures expertise. Focus optimizes resource usage. Focus clarifies the priorities for your business. Focus distinguishes you in the market. And focus demands awareness.

Cost leadership: a constant challenge

The strategy of cost leadership is dedicated to offering products to customers at costs lower than any competitor. Cost leadership is a strategy feasible within any quality level. In effect, it's value leadership at each level of quality. It's not as simple as being the company that cuts the most costs each year. That approach is more likely to eat away eventually at quality and ultimately hurt sales, so that you lack the funds you need to consistently innovate and come up with new ways of taking the cost out of your offerings.

> **Cost leadership is a strategy feasible within any quality level.**

There's one thing certain about cost leadership as a strategy. You'll always have competitors nipping at your heels. Cost advantages are often among the most easily copied, so cost leadership isn't a simple strategy. Instead, it's a strategy that demands constant innovation.

One innovation is the reshaping of value chains and the building of trust between suppliers and customers. Skanska, a leading

Swedish building contractor, looked to its value chain in its quest for cost leadership.

> **Skanska**
>
> Skanska was looking for ways to improve its competitiveness, in order to secure more market share in a declining market. It took two successful steps in this quest, each based on a different take on the same old practices. The first was its decision to impose some standardization where possible. Their intent was to save time and cost, both very important to customers. For example, while they would still customize elevator cabin interiors, Skanska worked with an elevator manufacturer and a number of architects and engineers to agree to five basic elevator cabin shells. No longer will each be a custom-made cabin. Standardization was virtually unheard of before Skanska made its move, yet the company was able to identify situations where standardization was possible without sacrificing the uniqueness of its property development projects: it now provides the same quality for its customers at lower cost. The second step was to negotiate sole supplier agreements with a number of its key suppliers, again with the goal of saving time and money. The open exchange of information these alliances fostered soon showed that the retailer, who in virtually all cases acted as the intermediary between the supplier and the contractor, was adding little value to the process. As a result, retailers fell out of the value chain for the majority of transactions with the supplier: again, unheard of in the industry to that point, but a real cost saver for both Skanska and the supplier, enabling Skanska to achieve its goal of increased competitiveness.[19]

Skanska was forced to innovate in order to find ways to squeeze the cost out of its offerings. The way to cost leadership was not through improving existing processes, but by finding new ways to approach the business.

Cost leadership is most obvious as a strategy in commodity type industries, where it's difficult to pursue the strategy of differentiated focus. But think about what that means. If you're in a commodity industry, you and most of your closest rivals will likely all be searching for the edge in cost. In the chemical industry, that's had some interesting results.

> ### The chemical industry
>
> As a commodity business, where economies of scale pay big dividends, chemical companies are motivated to build the biggest petrochemical plants possible and to run them at capacity. Bad news when two companies open mega-plants at the same time. Both will end up operating at less than capacity, and both will be less able to meet low cost than before. Two of the major players in the industry found a way around that. They built a factory together, each harvesting one non-competitive chemical from the factory.

These two competitors realized that the road to cost leadership lay in co-operation rather than conflict. It will be interesting to watch the repercussions of this new co-operation throughout the rest of the industry, or even in other industries.

The financial services industry is a new entrant into the commodity world. Everyone offers money, but who can make it available most inexpensively? Citibank pioneered customer-oriented technical innovation, such as automated banking, debit cards, and telephone banking and now these services have become the basic standard. That means that apart from the lending and savings rates which they charge and pay, there is little to differentiate banks. The ability to control costs is paramount. But the road to cost leadership is not a smooth one. There are many dimensions to which companies can look to reduce their costs: loan losses, efficiency in processing, or targeting customers with large deposits and few transactions, to name a few.

Adtranz

Adtranz, the company resulting from the January 1996 merger of ABB and Daimler-Benz' rail activities, is cost-focused, while taking a very aggressive approach in its quest for customer focus. Prices are eroding in the rail market, having dropped 30% in the two years preceding the merger. Throughout the industry companies are restructuring in an effort to provide the solutions the customer is demanding. Adtranz wants to gain a market edge by building the ability to customize low-cost solutions for all its customers. Multinational development teams, called Centres of Expertise (COE), work on modular product platforms which can be transferred to a number of markets, requiring only limited customization to meet local market requirements. Each technical solution is assessed to maximise the functions that can be adapted to more than one market. In this way, Adtranz can guard cost efficiencies while offering customized customer solutions. Each COE has global responsibility for its own product category. That means each COE has an interest in understanding the similarities and differences across all of its markets, so that products can be designed with maximum synergies. Adtranz shows us how a company can differentiate itself from its competitor by offering custom products, while at the same time keeping an eye on costs. It's a living example of a difficult balancing act: even if your strategy is one of focused differentiation, you just can't afford to ignore costs.

Cost means total cost to the customer, not just product cost. When companies are looking at their cost leadership potential, there may be locational advantages for some that outweigh the pure product cost advantages of others. For example, companies located in Europe may be able to overcome the disadvantage of their higher labour costs when dealing with their European customers, because they are local. The labour cost advantage of other nations is offset in part by the costs they incur in getting their products into the European market. The point is, look at the whole picture, so that you don't take on cost leadership as a strategy, only to find that one component of your costs renders you unable to compete effectively.

The feasibility of cost leadership for European companies depends on a number of things. It may be more feasible within

Europe itself than worldwide, because of the cost of doing business in Europe: regulation and its associated costs, labour cost and inflexibility. For the same reason, capital intensive industries in Europe are more likely to succeed with cost leadership strategies than are labour intensive industries. Germany has already seen a number of its companies send jobs to the east. Some European countries have made moves to at least increase the flexibility of their labour forces, and to hold the line on non-salary employee costs. But on the whole, given Europe's cost structure, niche and differentiation strategies may hold the most potential for European companies. Recall the Winterhalter story, *'small, even tiny, niche markets can become amazingly large when extended to the whole world.'*

Turn your attention to innovations that will allow you to reduce costs in ways that competitors will find difficult to imitate, but don't forget to be diligent in executing day-to-day activities. You may have come up with a cost innovation, but executing that innovation while letting other costs slide will wipe out your efforts. Operational excellence is the foundation of a cost leadership strategy, for two reasons. First, if you're not on top of execution, costs will rise and you won't be able to compete on the basis you intended to. Second, if poor execution means you sacrifice quality in order to get to the cost structure you need, you'll have inadvertently switched to a differentiation strategy, and one in which you're the loser. Your competitors will point to your lower quality level as a way to overcome your cost advantages.

The strategy of cost leadership reinforces the need to be able to excel at the day-to-day while at the same time keeping an eye to the future. You have to perfect your current operations and you have to see the future and understand technology so that you can identify the next improvement that will give you an edge.

Go for growth

'We successfully managed a turnaround and regained the trust of the financial markets by focusing on a growth strategy'

Companies are perpetually challenged to find ways of growing, not only relative to their own past performance, but relative to their competitors, and to search out growth into new fields which create new markets. A company that grows, but at a slower rate than its market, may be patting itself on the back for poor performance. Accidental, unfocused growth may be happy news in the short term, but can lead to dangerous ideas about the company's ability to compete. That's been a European problem. As consumer spending power increased, companies grew to meet the increased market size. They were very successful, not so much as a result of their own unique competitive advantages, but because each got a share of the growing amount of money being spent. That natural growth, fuelled by increased population and spending power, is slowing. Many European companies like Glaxo Wellcome, L'Oréal, Endesa, Promodès and Marchés Usines Auchan, however, have read the writing on the wall and have built sustainable competitive advantages that have helped them sustain growth.

Real growth means growth in value. Top-line growth that comes at a cost equal to the improved revenue isn't producing value for the company. We see growth building in a spiral. The first and easiest pickings come from cost control. Then comes top-line growth – the search for ways to increase revenue. Top-line growth combined with good cost control brings growth in profits. Sustainable growth in profits with sensible investment requirements leads to growth in value – the most important goal of any growth strategy.

Finally, a growth strategy positively impacts everyone in the firm. There's no comparison between the morale at a company that's growing and one that's shrinking. Don't underestimate the value of that boost in spirit. Restructuring for growth gets a better reception. People are more eager to build for the future than they are to tear down what they've already built.

Growth is the only option

Your strategy should aim for profitable growth. That's tough to dispute, but it's one of those things that companies forgot for a while. Most fell into thinking that the only way to compete was to cut, and a little while later, cut again. They are just now emerging from that trance. But the cost-cutting habit is a hard one to shake. Even those who claim their restructuring aimed to exploit market opportunities, implemented cost-cutting solutions and cost-focused performance measures. And the triggers that business leaders point to for the next round of restructuring are largely cost-focused as well.

The issue of cost control will never go away, but it should never be the centre of a company's thinking either. It's time to get past the idea that cost-cutting can solve all problems. The easy gains have been picked off. Most companies have reduced costs, cut lead times and re-engineered processes. While companies that missed those waves may have fallen away, most companies have gone through the necessary work of cost-cutting and re-engineering, only to find themselves still equal to their competitors.

Managers are concerned about the short-term results orientation of shareholders who, however, sacrifice growth for quick hits. They point to the positive reaction of the stock markets to news of downsizing.

Positive stock market reaction

A company's executives really believed that the downsizing they were proposing wouldn't be in the best long-term interest of the company, but, 'What can we do: the minute we announce this programme, our share price will go up'.

There is increasing evidence, though, that short-term pressure prevails only when the market does not have confidence in a company's long-term growth and value-creation prospects. One way to generate that confidence is to build early wins into your restructuring. These first successes are strong indicators that you know what you're doing and will achieve the plan you've laid out. That can help build patience in investors. At the same time, it's important to actively convince stakeholders of your company's growth potential. After all, if you don't exploit your potential, others will.

A company that can't find ways to grow faces a bleak future. European salaries continue rising, beyond the increase in the cost of living and despite recessionary times. Without top-line growth, companies will find their profits and prospects shrinking, and will find themselves less and less able to compete with those whose resources are increasing through growth.

Growth opens doors. Downsizing, by its very nature, closes them. If you can achieve profitable growth, you'll always be able to outperform pure cost-cutting.

Finding growth potential

New products. New geographies. New customers. These are the three basic sources of growth. Hybrids of these basics can lead to new value propositions and new marketing mixes – also fertile potential for growth. Which of these sources and how many of them to pursue depends on two things: market opportunities and competencies. Market opportunities can take many forms: buying groups that are increasing in wealth, technology changes, evolving tastes of existing market segments. What pressures are there for change, and how (including how quickly) can you capitalize on those pressures? Evaluate market opportunities in the light of competencies: can you offer what you've determined the market is looking for? Do you have relevant skills and experience? Or can you readily obtain and integrate those skills and resources?

The best growth strategies build on a company's successes and skills. That doesn't mean you can only grow by doing more of what you're doing now. But it does mean that you should try to grow into your strengths rather than expanding where your knowledge is limited. Look for ways to take advantage of what you're good at. Make focus a prerequisite of any growth strategy. Ahold, the Dutch food retailing giant, has used focus to become one of the top food retailers in the United States.

> **The best growth strategies build on a company's successes and skills.**

Ahold

Koninklijke (Royal) Ahold had sales of 16.4 billion ECU in 1996, and operates over 2000 supermarkets on four continents. Through carefully selected acquisitions, it has been able to increase revenues and profits substantially in an industry which is generally considered stagnant. Sales have grown 63% between 1992 and 1996, and net earnings have more than doubled over the same period. Ahold has chosen to grow by expanding in the line of business it knows best, grocery retailing. It's unconventional for food retailers to think as globally as Ahold has. But Ahold committed itself to a growth strategy. With close to a 30% share of the market in the Netherlands, and with exorbitant land prices and difficult planning procedures discouraging further expansion there, Ahold turned to new geographies to fulfil its growth ambitions. 'Our ambitious goal – to become the largest and most profitable international supermarket company – has come considerably closer to reality,' says president Cees van der Hoeven.

The company wants to build on its expertise and developed a mentoring system to assist in this regard: seasoned Ahold operating companies take special responsibility for assisting new ventures in emerging markets. As noted in the annual report: 'Through co-operation and knowledge transfer we are realizing important efficiencies and economies of scale ... A solid business base and detailed understanding of every aspect of its core business allows Ahold to move confidently and aggressively, whether in pursuit of growth opportunities, operating synergies or new and better ways of serving the customer.'

Ahold grows with focus and discipline. It chose to grow along the geographic and new customer (late night shopper) dimensions, but did so in a way that built on its core competencies and core business.

In marked contrast, think of the companies that have used their resources to expand into new fields where they lack expertise, only to divest a few years later.

> ### Herlitz International Trading
>
> In 1994 Herlitz International Trading, a major pulp and paper trading company, bought a 33% share of the Russian paper mill AO Volga – the future prospects of the Russian market looked too promising to pass up. And indeed, thanks to a buoyant market, Herlitz's investment developed nicely until 1996. But then things went awry. Paper prices on the international market dropped by 15 to 20%, while raw material costs and taxes went up. The result for Herlitz: Volga was costing 25 million ECU in cash just to sustain operations. Management at Herlitz International Trading finally gave in, in mid-1997, admitting its inability to handle management of a paper mill in Russia. While markets were strong, they could ride the wave, but faced with a business they didn't understand in a declining market and a business environment that was radically different from their own Western European one, they were out of their depth. The mill is closed for the moment, putting its 4000 employees on hold, and Herlitz is trying to sell its stake. Herlitz has learned its lesson, and is refocusing on its core business. Says Peter Herlitz, chairman of the board and partner: 'We had to learn that our shareholders felt irritated by the wide spectrum of activities we pursue. Herlitz needs to become a more reliable partner for its shareholders. Also the holding does not have the resources to guarantee growth in all segments.'

Other companies use profitable lines of business to prop up those that probably should never have been entered in the first place.

4 • Strategy demystified

Profitable and unprofitable lines of business

Looking for growth opportunities, a company that had built sustained success in the baking powder business expanded first into other food powders such as flavourings and puddings, but then turned to a vast range of unrelated businesses, including, among others, banking, shirt-making, writing paper, brewing, frozen food, luxury hotels and shipping companies. It continued to make good profits in its baking powder business, but large segments of its diversification were unsuccessful.

Grow with what you're good at. It may be your product, which you can sell to more people in more markets. It may be your method of distribution, so you can look for additional lines to distribute. Or it may be some other dimension. But looking outwardly is at least as critical as looking inwardly. Only by understanding the market and the people who will buy your product can you realistically assess your growth prospects. The baking powder company's diversification didn't seem to build on any particular market opportunity, just on purchase opportunities that had no real connection to its core operations. On the other hand, Ahold's understanding of its customers and potential customers led it to real growth successes.

The best growth strategies are those that shape your competencies into something your customer wants. Breakthroughs happen when you meet needs your customers may not have yet identified. One way to find those breakthroughs is to look beyond your own customer. Think about your customers' customers. What are their needs, and what interesting prospects are there for your customer to serve its market better? What would make your customer look good to its customers? The answers to those questions can shed light on ways to help your customers excel. And the more they grow, the more you grow.

Find growth by looking at the world in new ways. Really turn facts inside out to look for what true limitations they present and what breakthroughs they conceal. Get as many facts as you can. Remember to look outwardly and inwardly – developing strategy by ignoring one or the other guarantees important issues will go unaddressed. Digging for the true possibilities of the firm can uncover some hidden gems. Look at what the Bert Claeys group, a Belgian cinema operator, was able to accomplish by taking a new look at its industry:

Bert Claeys

'The Belgian cinema industry had been declining for more than three decades and was going through an industry shakeout in the late 1980s. As videos, cable and satellite TV came into homes and film distributors shortened the time between the release of a film at the cinema and on video, the fate of the industry seemed sealed. Acting on the assumption that industry conditions are a given, cinema operators tried to maximize their share of shrinking demand by splitting cinemas into multiple screens, improving marketing and avoiding large, fixed-cost investments. That is, all except Bert Claeys. Bert Claeys saw how its competitors' responses were abetting the downfall of the industry. With small screens, old seats, poor projection equipment, higher prices and lower choice than home entertainment, was it surprising that the industry was collapsing? Bert Claeys refused to accept that decline was irreversible and set out to put the magic back into cinema. It built Kinepolis, the world's first 'megaplex' with 25 screens and 7,600 seats. With wide screens, spectacular sound, comfortable seating, the best pick of blockbusters and easy parking, Bert Claeys not only won more than 50% of the Brussels' market in its first year, but revitalized the industry. Cinema demand increased by over 40% and the company achieved a profit margin that was double the industry average.'[20]

When every other company in the industry was focused on how to shrink the least, the Bert Claeys group found a way to grow, they didn't have different information than their competitors, they just interpreted it differently. The message is: don't accept limitations too readily. Turn the facts over one more time to see whether the limitation is in the way you are interpreting the facts, rather than in the facts themselves.

Another important way to uncover growth potential is to dissect new industry and technological breakthroughs. Think about their implications for industries and businesses other than those directly involved in the breakthrough. Where does the potential lie, and does a particular breakthrough in one industry mean death for others? Cloning and other genetic technologies have implications for a number of other industries, the most obvious of which are food and pharmaceuticals. Breakthroughs in data management can give companies a big jump on their competitors. Data mining, for example, helps refine understanding of customer habits. EDI (Electronic Data Interchange) can dramatically streamline logistics in any industry. And here's how L.M. Ericsson of Sweden exploited a technological niche to become a global player in telecommunications:

L. M. Ericsson

The emergence of electronic switching technology radically changed the cost structure in the niche in which Ericsson had been operating: developing countries and smaller European markets that lacked national suppliers and that used the same switching systems as the Swedish market. It appeared that individual electronic switching systems would require a large fixed-cost investment for each country, making the new technology too expensive for the smaller telephone systems that Ericsson relied upon for its business. Ericsson understood early what the implications of the new technology were for its business, and looked for ways to turn that technology to its advantage. The company developed modular software packages that allowed these smaller telephone companies to convert gradually, and that could be configured to meet the needs of different telephone companies at acceptable cost levels. Ericsson's growth flourished as the small telephone systems converted, and it gained a software cost and variety advantage that continually reinforces itself.[21]

The technologies can provide exciting growth opportunities. The very newness of these technologies means there are many ideas yet to be exploited. If you have the creativity and foresight to understand those opportunities both in the industry in which the technology has evolved, and even more so in other industries, growth opportunities will come your way.

Preparing the conditions for growth

Profitable growth usually doesn't happen magically. Having a great idea for growth doesn't help much if you haven't got the skills or resources to carry it out. And having resources won't lead to growth if you don't know where to direct them. An important first step to growth is putting your house in order. A company fighting for survival isn't a good candidate for growth. But companies with a good core of existing operations are, because those operations fund the growth initiatives, and they give stakeholders confidence in the company's ability to grow. Without that confidence, stakeholders become impatient with lengthy time horizons – the pressure to find short-term profit opportunities mounts at the expense of longer-term growth. A company in crisis needs to concentrate on survival – looking for growth in those circumstances could spell disaster.

Once your company is in shape, start anticipating new conditions and needed change. This approach – pro-active restructuring – lets you lead, rather than labour to catch up. And by having the right strategy at the right time, not only can you lead, you have the potential to redefine the business and completely change the rules in your industry – a sure-fire recipe for growth (see Figure 4.5).

Superior strategies redefine the industry

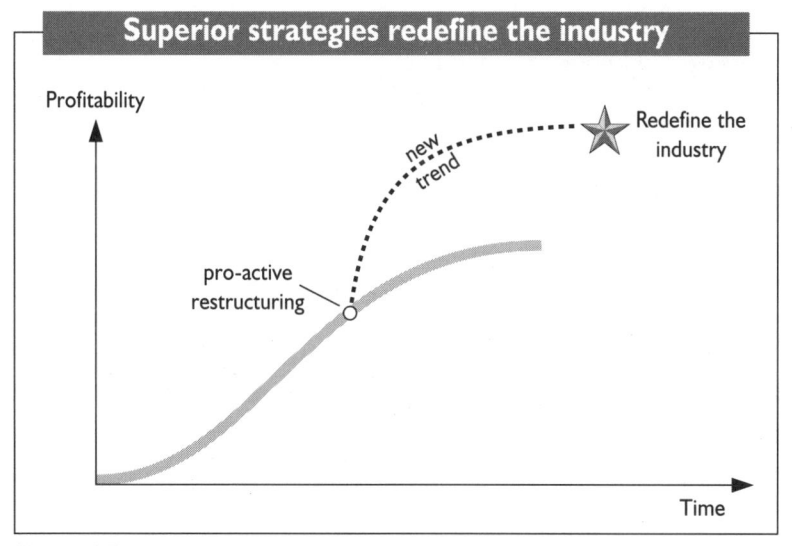

Figure 4.5

At the same time, get people in the mood to grow. Years of bottom-line focus can mean that people have completely stopped looking for ways to grow. Growth should be a priority, supported through your company's reward system and through the actions of top management. If you don't search for ways to grow, you can be almost certain growth won't happen.

Ahold

Ahold is a company in the mood to grow. It defines itself to its customers, employees and shareholders in those terms, and everyone believes growth is possible. Every speech the president makes talks about its goals and achievements in the realm of growth. Its vision is to grow quickly and profitably to become the world's leading supermarket company. Even in the Netherlands, a mature market, the company managed to increase its sales 4.4% and its operating profit 14% over 1996/97.

Think about the mindset in your company, and look for ways to open up thinking and generate confidence in the future.

> **Skanska**
>
> Skanska, the innovative Swedish building contractor we met earlier, launched its soul-searching, which led to significant breakthroughs, when one of its board members noted that the cost curve for the building industry had not gone down with experience as it did in other industries such as the automotive industry. His questioning of why that was so led the company to look at its business in ways it had never done before. He led the way in altering the company's mindset.[22]

The message: think ahead to what resources your strategy implies.

Recognize too that growth puts all kinds of stresses on your company. In anticipation of growth, think about what it will take to make the strategy a reality in terms of skills, infrastructure, culture and other resources. If the resources you need to achieve growth aren't available, or are underestimated, the growth won't happen, or it could happen at the expense of other parts of your business. The message: think ahead to what resources your strategy implies.

Aim for relevance

Your goal: to design the best strategy you can for increasing your company's value. Best in practical terms. A challenging strategy that forces people out of a 'business as usual' mindset, but not one that just isn't possible to implement.

Test the strategy: what outcomes will it deliver?

A well-thought-out strategy doesn't just identify an opportunity, it tests that opportunity against possible outcomes to make sure it has staying power and a good chance of success. That's the best use for many of the frameworks that consultants and academics advocate: portfolio planning, strategic gameboard, value chain analysis, the McKinsey Seven S framework, the Boston Consulting matrix. They all suggest ways to come up with strategic options and issues. We take a closer look at just two of those techniques to show how to capture their value.

Scenario building

It starts by getting everyone to think differently about strategy. The typical strategic planning process focuses on finding one right answer – the single best strategy. You make a range of assumptions about the future, all based on the same basic business conditions. With scenario building, in contrast, you look at a range of completely new different business conditions: what could happen in the industry – with customers, with competitors, with suppliers? Each scenario is given the same weight. Strategies are developed and tested against each set of circumstances, to determine which strategy is the strongest, on balance, against the possible futures for the company. Shell demonstrates the value of scenario building:

Shell

In the 1960s, Shell's scenario building process led the company to question what might happen with future oil supply. Everyone had always assumed that the limit to supply was the ability to find and extract oil. In thinking about different ways the industry could evolve, one executive mused that the governments in oil-producing countries could take a larger role and start controlling the supply of oil available to the major oil companies. It was a completely radical thought, but once the idea was put forward, Shell decided it really was a possible future. No more or less likely than the *status quo*, but

> nevertheless worthy of consideration. Three outcomes followed the inclusion of this scenario in Shell's thinking: first, the strategy they developed could fare well both in existing supply situations, and in the eventuality that the supply became limited. Second, they really thought through the implications of this scenario, and developed ideas about what specific moves to make if it came true. Finally, having thought about this scenario in advance, the company recognized the developments in the Middle East as the energy crisis scenario they had been discussing, and were able to shift gears quickly. They were the first to react, and the best equipped to react, and therefore came through the oil crisis in much better shape than competitors.[23]

Scenario-building acknowledges that the future can't be known with certainty, and seeks to develop strategy that makes sense under a range of assumptions. The process itself forces companies out of the habit of assuming the future won't be very different from the past, and forces everyone into thinking about what *could* be different, either because of the company's own actions or due to uncontrollable circumstances.

Strategic dynamics

Another technique gaining popularity with European managers is strategic dynamics, built on the systems dynamics approach re-popularized by Peter Senge. Its goal is to help you understand the implications of strategies you consider, and to better focus the development of strategy in the first place. Strategic dynamics looks at the company as a living changing system rather than as a static aggregation of parts. That ensures interrelationships between different parts of the system are identified – not just that the left hand knows what the right hand is doing, but that if the left hand does x, the right kneecap will respond with y. It's a way of surfacing everyone's assumptions about how the business operates. Through strategic dynamics, you can discuss, integrate, and test the consistency of your mental models; review your assumptions about your business; simulate the impact of possible decisions; and, most importantly, uncover the unintended consequences of decisions you plan to make.

Traditional problem-solving teaches that the best way to solve a problem is to break it into its component parts. Strategic dynamics concentrates on interrelationships and how the system works as a whole. It overcomes the danger of finding a solution to one problem, in isolation, and inadvertently creating a new problem. The outcome is better, more informed decisions about the future.

Swedish mobile phone operator

A Swedish mobile phone operator used strategic dynamics to simulate the interactions between customers, clients, competitors and regulatory authorities. Through mapping the business system, management got a deeper look at the fundamental structures and connections. Until then, their power over the future of the industry was little understood. With strategic dynamics, the business strategy was changed significantly and capital expenditures were phased in more gradually than originally planned. Moreover cost savings potential was identified that the company hadn't spotted before the strategic dynamics process got underway.

Our thoughts on the myriad of management frameworks? Most of them can provide good tests of the staying power of your strategy in a variety of circumstances. But they can't replace knowledge of customer, market, industry and the future, so don't go too deep into the jungle. Keep strategy development simple, and keep it aimed at relevant considerations.

Balance competing drives to gain buy-in

Your strategy should consider the three competitive drives within the firm (see Figure 4.6). The task is to balance these three dimensions. A strategy that doesn't achieve that balance needs more work. The firm's foundations are its investors, resources and customers. You must deliver value to all three. Each needs a reason to commit to the company, or they will find other firms that can better meet their needs.

- **Competition for investment:** to deliver value to owners by ensuring that business portfolios are worth more than the sum of their parts.
- **Competition for resources:** to match resources with objectives, by delivering enough value to attract and retain quality employees, suppliers and technologies.
- **Competition for customers:** to gain competitive advantage by delivering superior value to customers.

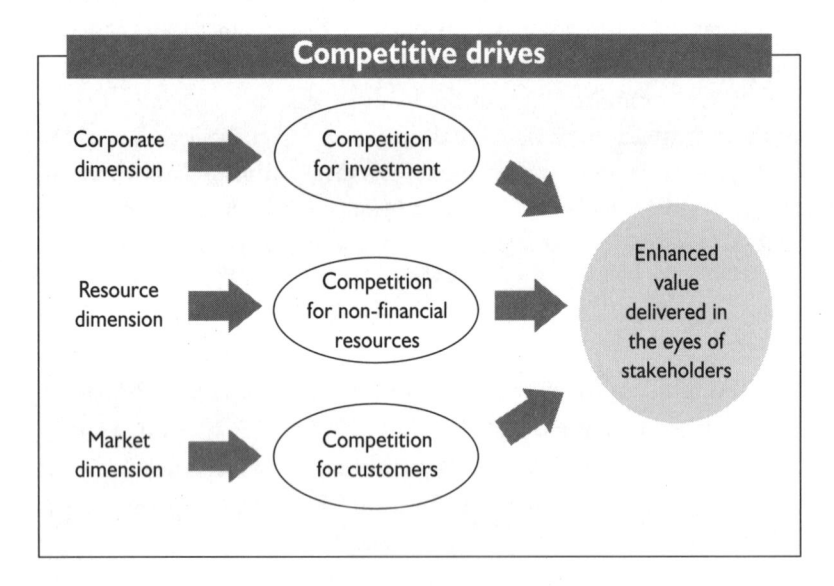

Figure 4.6

Saatchi & Saatchi

When Saatchi & Saatchi failed to satisfy its owners in the 1980s, the owners took steps to gain more operational control. In doing so, they obliged corporate managers to act as business level managers, thus alienating key account executives, several of whom became disenchanted and left. Customers saw management was being run by owners rather than for customers and switched to other agencies, including a new agency established by some of the former Saatchi executives. Consequently, the share price collapsed and a chain of events initiated by dissatisfied owners caused such dissatisfaction among stakeholders and customers that a substantial amount of owner value was destroyed.

Successful balancing act

The automotive parts manufacturer we described in the second case study of this chapter performed a successful balancing act. Its strategy resulted in an improved bottom line for its investors, improved cost and focus for its customers, and launched new growth that appealed to its suppliers and employees.

In a post-merger situation, the issues are even more urgent. How can you ensure that key people decide to stay with the newly merged company? And what implications will the merger have on your ability to deliver services?

> ### Misinformation and confusion
>
> A recent acquisition of an adhesive label manufacturer by a much larger company in the same business in a different country was clouded in misinformation and confusion. Employees of the acquired company were left in the dark. Many became fed up and left, to the delight of the new owners who were convinced they were in charge and didn't really need the old guys any more. The new parent company soon found itself in the embarrassing position of having only one, somewhat alienated, salesperson who could communicate with the largely French, German and Dutch speaking customers in their native languages. Sales and morale have continued to fall, and it's unclear whether the purchasing company will realize any of the benefits it anticipated when it made its acquisition.

Activate a sensor system

A sensor system, scanning the horizon for threats and opportunities, is an invaluable source of information when generating strategic options. It's essential to be in touch with your environment, and to have an understanding of the implications that changes in that environment have for your company. In today's climate – where change is increasing in frequency and intensity – not having some kind of early warning system could be fatal. A company should always be testing new visions and new looks at the world. Will your plans still take you towards a differentiated competitive position, or is it time to change direction? Acting as an on-going source of market, economic, and internal intelligence, the sensor system provides focus for strategy discussions by highlighting issues which the strategy should address. What could derail your plans? Is there anything happening externally that you need to adapt to? What about within your company?

An effective sensor system relies on people at all levels in the organization – not just top management, nor the front lines alone. And an effective sensor system has a control tower: there's somewhere to go with the information that's been collected, and the information gets used, not filed.

Market leader

A regional market leader in snow ploughing and road grading equipment carefully tracked its results for each sales effort by logging who its competitors were and which company's bid was successful. It also tracked the buying frequency of all prospective customers so that it would know when a sales opportunity was nearing. The company's percentage of winning bids dipped at the same time that one of its competitors began consistently winning bids, and just before a large number of sales opportunities were due. In response, the company launched an immediate, independent investigation into the purchase process of its customers as well as a customer evaluation of the main players in the market. The results led the company to reorient its sales process and upgrade its product, thereby reclaiming its position as market leader.

The road grader manufacturer capitalized on the information generated by its sensor system to revise its strategy for maintaining market leadership. It learned that its customers were expecting a more formalized selling process and more customized equipment than had been the case in the past. Rather than waiting for annual or quarterly reports, it collected, analyzed and acted on information as it became available.

> Synthesizing intelligence is a critical facet of successful strategy development.

Many companies have elaborate, state of the art, MIS systems and other intelligence gathering procedures, but that's not enough. The benefits of the sensor system accrue only to those who *use* the information. Our experience shows that many companies don't get beyond the collection stage, or if they do, they refuse to act on what the information is telling them. There's often an unexpressed hope that if they ignore the issues, these issues will disappear.

Rather than take this head-in-the-sand approach, use the information to guide your efforts. How large will the impact of perceived opportunities or threats be? How probable? Answering these questions will enable you to focus on those issues that are high probability and high impact. Synthesizing intelligence is a critical facet of successful strategy development.

IN BRIEF

Strategy

- Restructuring a company should no longer be an emergency matter executed under pressure. Companies should move into an elective restructuring mode by anticipating developments and overall strategic thinking.

- To refrain from strategy impostors like benchmarking, re-engineering and pure cost reduction, choices have to be made – but whatever the strategy, cost pressure will always remain an issue.

5

Emphasis on action

Turning strategy into reality

- Let Spearheaders be your frontmen
- Orient the stakeholders
- Conduct for speed
- Set and sustain the cadence of restructuring
- Keep your eye on the ball

'Lack of leadership during implementation was the biggest obstacle to our restructuring'

'Contradictions and delays hampered the implementation of our restructuring'

'New culture needs time – not enough time for implementation'

'Decision time lags hurt our restructuring'

5 • Emphasis on action

Once a company has defined its strategy, and the resulting restructuring it demands, the challenge shifts to implementing the changes that will yield the new, improved company. But grim statistics of restructuring failures prove it's not easy to shed the old and let the new emerge. Figuring out that you need to restructure is important. Figuring out what plan has the best potential for enhancing your company's value is vital. But those two steps are meaningless unless you can bring them to fruition, and that seems to be a problem for a lot of companies.

> **Figuring out what plan has the best potential for enhancing your company's value is vital.**

Implementing a restructuring involves understanding a web of interconnected factors and relationships. It requires big picture understanding combined with critical attention to detail (see Figure 5.1): experience, sensitivity, and determination are the key ingredients. Restructurings need to be fine-tuned as they proceed – with a keen eye to end goals.

Orchestrating a restructuring demands undivided attention

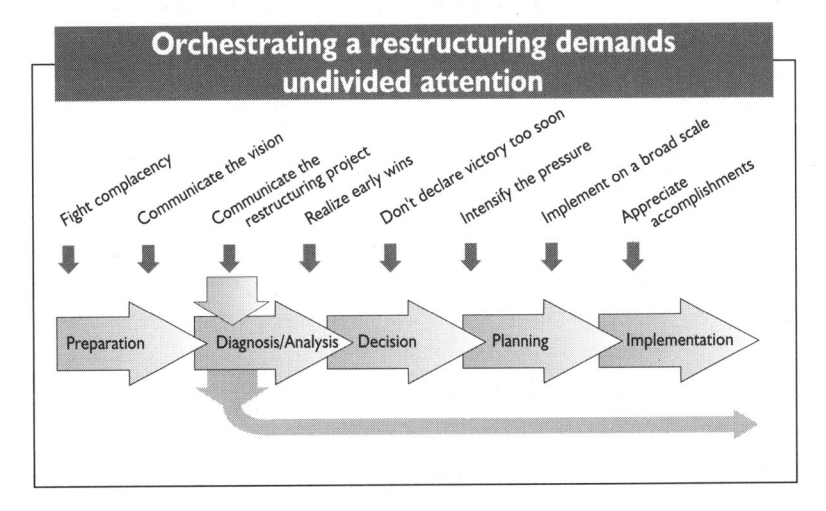

Fight complacency · Communicate the vision · Communicate the restructuring project · Realize early wins · Don't declare victory too soon · Intensify the pressure · Implement on a broad scale · Appreciate accomplishments

Preparation → Diagnosis/Analysis → Decision → Planning → Implementation

Figure 5.1

Turning strategy into reality means you need to clearly assess your starting point and what it will take to get the job done. That assessment involves internal and external stakeholders as well as the key team who will drive your restructuring to success. What will it take in terms of resources, human and other? Who do you need to persuade about the necessity of the restructuring, and what's in it for them?

Let Spearheaders be your frontmen

The first job for Spearheaders is to change the mindset of a whole company. However, in the course of the actual restructuring project they are just as important for the more operational and tedious tasks that implementing restructuring requires.

Spearheaders should not only be able to actively influence the (often) complacent mindsets of employees, they also have an active role in implementation. They are the doers. When we say it is critical that all stakeholders are informed of, and oriented about, the restructuring, that's the job of Spearheaders. They are the ones to talk to all levels in and maybe even outside the company about problems and how they can be solved. If an immediate solution is not possible, they have to come back to the people. A process of constant information and feedback develops. When you put the appropriate people in place (see *Chapter 3*) the chance of a restructuring failing will diminish considerably. But be aware of the fact that these people have to be special: energized and motivated, knowledge- and people-oriented.

Take care of all these things before you settle on your final restructuring plan. It's as important to make sure the company is capable of carrying out a plan as it is to understand whether, in ideal circumstances, the plan could deliver a company of improved value. Identify both the capabilities that are critical to transform the company, and those needed to run the company in its newly transformed state.

A restructuring, well-orchestrated by leaders and Spearheaders, takes place quickly and leaves the company and the people in good shape for day-to-day operations and future restructuring efforts. It's a matter of weaving together the people and the processes, and of understanding what needs to be done at each point in the restructuring. It's not a rigid set of steps that you plan at the outset. It's a fluid, dynamic process that adapts to circumstances as it proceeds, never losing sight of the ultimate goals.

Orient the stakeholders

We've talked about the need to balance the competing interests of stakeholders when developing strategy. It's important to keep them in mind as you restructure as well. That means first identifying which stakeholders have an interest in the restructuring. It's useful to think of three groups of people:

- Who is essential to the success of the organization?
- Who will be of significant help to the organization?
- Who is not directly involved but should be kept informed?

This classification of stakeholders can save time and energy throughout the restructuring. Knowing upfront whose concerns are most important can allow you to tailor the restructuring accordingly. All stakeholders do not need equal attention; choose which stakeholders to emphasize depending on the situation.

Siemens

For most of its history, the Siemens AG ignored its shareholders, because it could fund its activities with bank loans and retained earnings. Profits didn't seem important. That, plus the fact that the company was Germany's largest employer, prompted Jack Welch, CEO of General Electronic, to dismiss Siemens as being more of an employment office than a company. Now, however, to compete on a global scale, Siemens has to go beyond its traditional sources of funding. It will need to rely on the stock market, and therefore needs to demonstrate its profitability. Siemens has assessed its stakeholders and recognized that shareholders and capital markets will have greater impact on the company's ability to operate, and is adapting its strategy accordingly by increasing the emphasis on profits. As we noted earlier, the emphasis on profits is backed up by the companies revamped performance appraisal system.[24]

For example, in the automotive industry the tendency is much more towards recognizing and managing suppliers than in the financial services industry. That difference reflects the extent to which the automotive industry is governed by partnerships and alliances with suppliers.

Those internal to the company, plus customers, tend to be the stakeholders receiving the most attention. In contrast, in most situations, very little attention is paid to governments, creditors and the larger community. The message is that it's important to know *which* stakeholders to address. Those generally considered less important could have significant relevance in a particular restructuring. A company on the brink of financial collapse, for example, would probably elevate creditors and shareholders to key stakeholder status. As a general rule, however, internal stakeholders will always be of primary importance – the question is who gets added to that list.

Start by understanding stakeholder objectives: anticipate what they are looking for from your organization, how they will measure whether or not they have received it, and within what time horizon they are operating. Don't forget that your customers and suppliers may be important stakeholders, and don't limit yourself to your existing stakeholders – think about the changing composition of the group.

Your understanding of your stakeholders' objectives will help you assess how your restructuring plan will be perceived by them in terms of:

- the impact of their reaction
- the plan's acceptability (its fit with their objectives)
- their belief in its achievability
- their probable reaction.

If you want to know what your stakeholders are worried about, ask them directly. Think about the impact their reaction could have on your efforts. If it could render you unable to carry out the restructuring, the restructuring plan needs revision. Early negotiations with 'do or die' stakeholders can help reduce, or at least quantify, the degree of risk taken on in the restructuring.

Negotiating with stakeholders

For mergers between professional service firms, the challenge is ensuring that millions of ECU worth of highly mobile assets don't walk out the door before the merger has time to prove itself. In one such merger, the key stakeholders were identified as the top partners from around the globe. Acceptable buy-in was set at a minimum 90% yes vote for the merger. The belief was that with below 90% acceptance, a critical percentage of the company could be disaffected and undermine the merger.

In this case, identifying the risk and involving the key stakeholders early on ensured maximum commitment in a high risk situation.

Involve internal stakeholders early

Ask anyone, and they'll tell you people are their most important resource. When it comes to restructuring, the story is the same. Even though involvement and commitment of top management and employees are often cited as vital factors for success, we are a little sceptical about how far this is adhered to in practice. Employees may be important, but often not important enough, it appears, to involve them in the restructuring process. Executives reported *'confusion and animosity from managers and employees as they had not been involved'* and *'employee commitment was lacking, as only late in the project employees got involved.'*

These reactions corroborate what we see every day. Employees are *said* to be important, but top management doesn't live up to the implications of that.

> **What new strategic plan?**
>
> A European consumer goods manufacturer was holding an annual seminar for its top two levels of country managers. As part of the meeting, the organizers introduced the chairman, who began enthusiastically speaking about the company's new strategic plan. His audience looked on, dumbfounded. What new strategic plan? The questions slowly emerged, and the chairman realized that the strategy he had developed with a small staff team had never really sought input from or been explained to these managers.

Not much thought was given to how to involve and communicate with the country managers – the potential of their input was ignored. Ask the chairman what he meant by the importance of employees before the meeting, and his understanding of the same concept after the meeting. Quite a difference. The existence of the seminar was an indication that thought had been given to the importance of involving employees, but that involvement had more of a special event status, it was really not in the chairman's mindset on a day-to-day basis.

Our restructuring Affinity Council triggered lively debate about when and how best to involve employees, but our research was clear: fast restructurers involved their people to a much greater extent early in the process. They minimized employee involvement in decision-making, and had very high levels of involvement in implementation. In contrast, slow restructurers delayed until decision or even implementation before really involving employees.

Employees who help identify problems, typically commit to help solve them. They like knowing that senior executives and the Spearheaders solicit their ideas and respect their opinions. When employees buy in upfront, project leaders have the luxury of choosing the most appropriate project implementers. That relieves the pressure of trying to involve too many people in implementation, since support is already there.

Excluding middle management

The management of a financial institution described their restructuring: the entire process of analysis, strategy and decision making was purposely carried out behind closed doors. The result: failure, because middle management was completely alienated and refused to come on board for the project's implementation.

Attempting to involve employees in implementation without having involved them in the thought process that led up to it makes the restructuring process more difficult.

The necessary skills and resources must be available

There's nothing more frustrating for employees than being urged to carry out a project for which there are insufficient or inappropriate resources, skills, and infrastructure. The Spearheaders, early in the restructuring planning, should assess the capabilities crucial to turning the company into the one envisaged and those needed to operate the company once it is transformed. To understand the organization's existing capabilities, the following should be considered:

Spearheading Growth

- How much experience do the organization and its individuals have in undergoing the sort of change planned? What caused past successes and failures?
- How much experience do the organization and its people have in operating in the way that the new situation will demand? What caused past successes and failures?
- How successfully have people been able to learn and adapt to new skills and new ways of working?

> **The analysis of past successes and failures, in particular, will help you understand how to best use existing resources.**

One of the tricks is figuring out what people are really capable of. In most cases they can do more than they've shown the company. The Spearheaders will need a good understanding of how to nurture a mindset that ensures all the relevant talents in the organization are brought to bear on the restructuring. One of the hidden assets to keep in mind is the credibility that existing employees may have, especially relative to newcomers. That credibility within the organization can sometimes outweigh some shortfalls in specific experience.

The analysis of past successes and failures, in particular, will help you understand how to best use existing resources. Once it's clear what's possible with the people in place, it will also be clear what new resources you will need.

Checking capabilities

The steel mill engineering company we first met in *Chapter 3* assessed the market and its abilities and realized that its distinctive capabilities were its knowledgeable employees. The company decided that the package it should offer included engineering insight and design together with construction management. Comparing this strategy to the company's skills showed a shortfall in project management skills. The company launched a programme to upgrade those skills, to ensure its ability to carry out its strategy.

The company addressed the gap between the people it had and the people it would need to have to make its new strategy a success, and identified the skills and capabilities it needed to build in order to be able to operate as envisaged. Think about the change process itself, and what you need to make it succeed, but think beyond it too. The short-term priority is ensuring that the company can accomplish the restructuring, but following right on its heels are the requirements for operating the transformed company.

If you've got the wrong people, admit it.

Evaluating the salesforce

A European manufacturer of GSM mobile handsets was quick to understand the impact of the new international GSM standard: new, giant competitors such as Motorola, Nokia and Ericsson, and a big change in the customer base. The manufacturer's best customers would be large and sophisticated service providers that themselves were full-service consultant-suppliers to end-users. No longer would most sales be made to small and medium-sized retailers. The salesforce now needed to excel in dealing with the professional buyer serving mass markets, not with the needs of the little guy. In this new competitive environment, top management quickly assessed the company's existing capabilities and concluded that new sales skills were critical, and there wasn't time to develop all those skills internally. They evaluated the salespeople, keeping those they felt would adapt most readily to the new customer base, and brought in new salespeople with proven skills in working the professional service providers. They correctly recognized that there was no point in developing a new sales strategy if they didn't follow through to make sure the company had the people it needed to carry out that strategy.

We've seen many restructuring projects go wrong when the key restructuring team is made up of top management's old cronies, who are not right for the job. The organization interprets that as a sign that nothing has really changed. The other mistake we see is people being put in charge of restructuring because they have outlived their usefulness in day-to-day operations. On the surface it's an ideal solution, but it doesn't make sense to put responsibility for change in the hands of the people most interested in the *status quo*.

The new company that emerges on the other side of the restructuring will be designed to excel in its expected market situation. One of the most difficult aspects of designing that future structure is figuring out the starting point. It takes some serious digging. Sure, the organization chart shows formal reporting structure and lines of authority in the company, but *how does it really work?*

Evaluating the actual structure in the light of both the restructuring plan and the redesigned organization will highlight where changes are needed. In general, companies need to realign their structures to shift emphasis to the market side of the business. The internal cost side has received lots of attention. The structures that safeguard cost control and efficient production and logistics should not be sacrificed in favour of market-driven structures. Rather they should be folded into the new structure. In designing organizational structure, division of duties usually gets lots of attention. Just as important, however, is the coordination of responsibilities. The organizational structure should promote effective sharing of responsibilities and information.

Keep critical stakeholders 'in the loop': communicate

We've talked about the importance of communication, especially with internal stakeholders like employees and middle management. Without that communication, and without real effort at enthusing and involving these individuals, they most likely won't develop the mindset you're relying on for your restructuring. But in your quest to get internal people on board, don't forget important external stakeholders. Think about what information they will need and want. And think about when they will want it. Their interest doesn't end with the announcement of the project – their interest in progress and results will parallel yours. Depending on the situation, the failure to involve a workers' council for example, or a lender, at a critical stage could derail your entire restructuring.

The segmentation of stakeholders guides the frequency and type of communication. Who needs to be actively involved in the process, and who just needs progress reports? As a general rule, more is better, and the ability to handle two-way communication will benefit both senior management and the stakeholders. Their feedback on progress is an important input into the evolution of the restructuring. For anyone whose support you need in order to make the restructuring a success, too much information is generally better than too little. In the case of the workers' council, or trade union, for example, whoever you are dealing with knows they will be faced with all kinds of questions from your employees. Your goal should be to make them so well informed that they can easily answer all those questions. And other external stakeholders can also influence a company's ability to restructure. European companies frequently face governments that want their needs met in order to co-operate in privatization programmes, and other restructuring that affects what they view as 'national' industries. For example, in a number of recent instances, the government of France has put pressure on companies to act in a certain way, which the government believes is in the best interest of its people, despite the companies' wishes to get on with restructuring.

Spearheading Growth

> ### Government pressure
>
> A recent example of government pressure is reflected in Christian Blanc's decision to step down as chairman of Air France. Blanc has confronted the French government on numerous occasions in his tenure as chairman of the airline, but finally gave up when he realized that the government would not consent to privatizing a majority share of the airline. 'In the ruthlessly competitive battle among airlines worldwide, the clocks are ticking away. There is no time to lose. It is precisely on this crucial point, the pace of our development, that there is a disagreement with the shareholder.'[25]

In Air France's case, a disagreement with the shareholder meant that the company couldn't carry out the restructuring it wanted to, and the chairman threw in the towel as a result. That shows the power external stakeholders can have over a company's future. Two things could have improved the situation. Had Air France been able to make a stronger case about their belief in the benefits of privatization, the crucial stakeholder – the government – might have been brought on board. A tough situation for Air France given the recent socialist election victory. The other change could come on the part of the shareholders: slowly more and more governments are becoming convinced of the benefits of privatization, but the road is a long and difficult one.

The rules about communication apply no matter what kind of story you have to tell. Bad news doesn't disappear. There's a real temptation to keep bad news about a restructuring's progress hidden, in the hopes that it will correct itself and the dirty secret never sees the light of day. That's a dangerous choice, because experience shows that the earlier stakeholders are informed about deviations from the plans they have seen and approved, the greater is the likelihood that they will continue to support the restructuring. Especially if the report also includes how to address the deviation to get the restructuring back on a successful track.

Keep your ear to the ground in both a formal and informal way to see whether stakeholders are reacting to your messages in the way you had expected. Analyze their reactions and use this information to modify your restructuring plan or to identify what you can do to address stakeholder concerns. Be sure to differentiate between reactions that are caused by a misunderstanding of the information you've conveyed and those that result from the content of the message.

Conduct for speed

There's a mistaken impression that pushing for speed means sacrificing results. We disagree. You don't have to choose one or the other. In fact you *shouldn't*. Accelerating the speed while keeping an eye on results is the best way to implement restructuring. Top performers took 30% less time to restructure than the rest, and they provide strong evidence that restructuring with speed is the way to go (see Figure 5.2).

Top performers spend 30% less time in the restructuring process

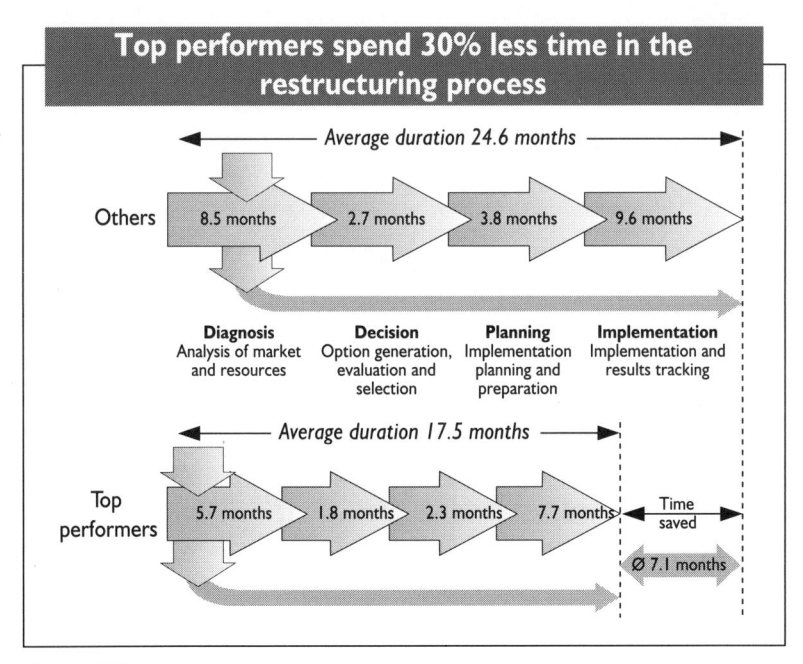

Others — Average duration 24.6 months
8.5 months → 2.7 months → 3.8 months → 9.6 months

Diagnosis	Decision	Planning	Implementation
Analysis of market and resources	Option generation, evaluation and selection	Implementation planning and preparation	Implementation and results tracking

Top performers — Average duration 17.5 months
5.7 months → 1.8 months → 2.3 months → 7.7 months → Time saved
Ø 7.1 months

Figure 5.2

Why is it important to restructure quickly? The sooner you complete your restructuring, the sooner you'll benefit from improved results. Look at what's happened to two telecom companies who started on similar paths.

Telefónica and Telecom Italia/Stet

Both Telefónica and Telecom Italia/Stet set out to privatize their operations. Telefónica carried out its privatization quickly and decisively, by starting out with some rationalization to get the cost base in line and then adding some new ventures to balance risks. They secured shareholdings in a number of Latin American telecom companies, and formed an alliance with British Telecom, MCI and Portugal Telecom. Telefónica's privatization was concluded in early 1997, with shares being sold and management changing from government to independent agents (although the Spanish government will retain some veto rights for a period of time). The company's share price has increased by 25% from February to August 1997.

Things worked differently at Telecom Italia. Efforts to privatize have been stalled because of political conflicts of interest. A merger of Stet and its operational subsidiary, Telecom Italia, was carried out as a prerequisite for privatization. The State share is now about 45%, but the treasury department retained a number of special privileges, including the right to veto privatization plans. In fact, the legal basis for privatization is not yet available. Bureaucracy and political delays make it unclear when the privatization will finally and fully get underway.

If you can restructure more quickly than your competitors, you'll have the time and energy to get even further ahead of them. Telefónica is clearly in a better position to exploit opportunity than Telecom Italia. Restructurers also pointed to the business environments as a reason to get faster:

'The world will continue changing very fast and corporations need to be aware of it and be prepared to adapt themselves to this changing environment.'

Rapid technology development and price performance means the lead time between identifying competitor action and its implementation is becoming shorter.

Working to tight deadlines ensures that the restructuring momentum continues. There's usually significant effort involved in launching a restructuring, especially in the time and energy spent getting people on board. Keeping the project moving helps keep those people enthused. They will be able to see progress. Their belief in their ability and the company's ability to succeed will strengthen. In contrast, a restructuring that is subject to delay and second guessing will soon lose supporters. Our survey respondents pointed to loss of momentum as a barrier to restructuring success:

> *'Partly restructuring, ending in the middle, causes serious damage.'*

and:

> *'Keeping the momentum and speed was difficult – management tried to slow down implementation.'*

Think of restructuring as getting an aeroplane into the air – there's a lot of energy used up in achieving lift off, and steady fuel needed once the 'plane' is in the air. If the fuel is cut off, the plane crashes. The effort of keeping it going is much less than the pain of dealing with the crash. And the time saved will translate into an improved bottom line.

The importance of speed and momentum increases as forces for change increase. Restructuring plans are based on the market and competitive conditions the company faces. If restructuring takes too much time, or loses momentum, a project can become obsolete before you complete it. It pays to work fast to realize the benefits of restructuring more quickly and to ensure that the restructuring retains its relevance.

Some industries seem to have learned this lesson better than others: the average automotive restructuring took only 17 months, while manufacturers of investment goods took 29 months.

Make decisions, not delays

The decision to restructure, and the decision of how best to accomplish the restructuring's goals are the tip of the iceberg. As you implement your plans, you will need to make many more decisions. These will be made within the company's clearly developed strategy, and so should not result in delay. However, in practice, we find that a sort of restructuring paralysis sometimes takes hold. Management is unable to make the decisions required to get from one restructuring phase to the next.

> **Delay**
>
> A company in the machinery industry was discussing the merits of a proposed restructuring project. Even after they were shown that every day of delay in making the decision to proceed was costing them 130,000 ECU, they weren't able to push forward their plans for almost two months. They did finally decide to restructure – obviously with diminished results, because they couldn't recover the money lost during the delay.

This reluctance to make decisions is something we come across frequently in our restructuring work, and we asked participants in our Restructuring Affinity Council to explain the causes (see Figure 5.3). Of them, 60% indirectly admitted to being afraid to make a decision: 'anxiety created by fearing the consequences' and 'need to establish a safe base'. They weren't completely sure of the consequences of restructuring, or they were worried about securing their own positions before moving ahead. In effect, they admitted to the cowardice we identified earlier as a deterrent to a winning restructuring mindset. But doing nothing is also a decision, and often a dangerous one, because it's a decision for which you haven't really thought through the consequences. Once you've committed to a restructuring project, don't let it wither away because you've been hit by an attack of nerves.

5 • Emphasis on action

Why is excessive time spent making decisions between the phases of restructuring ?

- 33% Need to establish a safe base for the key people
- 28% Lack of buy-in from critical stakeholders
- 27% Anxiety created by fearing the consequences
- 11% Interim results reduce the necessary pressure

Source: Restructuring Affinity Council

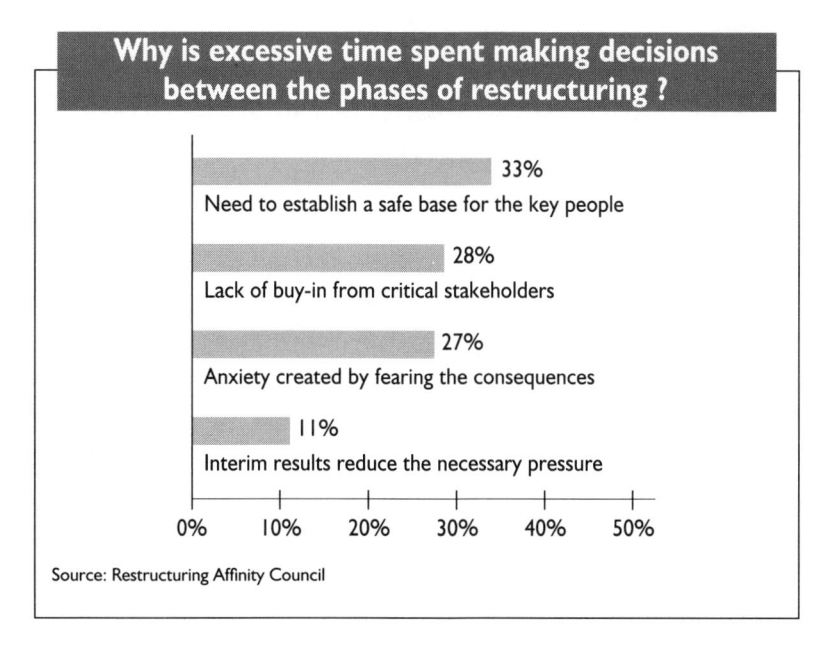

Figure 5.3

In the very early planning stages of restructuring, the primary consideration is whether restructuring is necessary at all. Most will try to understand and compare the results expected from sticking to the *status quo* with anticipated restructuring results. Will the company be able to improve its competitive position through restructuring, resulting in greater value? Are there threats that *cannot*, or opportunities that *should not*, be ignored if you want to maximize the company's value? Overlaid on all of this is the optimal timing for carrying out the restructuring. Is it best to proceed immediately, or can more value be generated by waiting until certain conditions change? As the restructuring proceeds and you are plagued with uncertainty, turn to that analysis. There wouldn't be a restructuring at all if there weren't very convincing arguments in favour.

> Is it best to proceed immediately, or can more value be generated by waiting until certain conditions change?

Analyze properly but speedily

It's necessary to do some thinking upfront about what the key drivers and issues are for the options under consideration, so that you can carry out an effective, to-the-point analysis. The goal for each decision should be a workable database that allows you to test some clearly formulated hypotheses, and come to a quick conclusion. No matter how much work you do, there's no way to have all the factors identified and properly weighted. Rather than search for elusive perfection, it's better to do swift and strong analysis, and then move forward.

Austrian electrical engineering company

An Austrian electrical engineering company spent seven months analyzing the synergies in a planned merger with a competitor. The extensive analysis uncovered so many uncertainties and created so many doubts that the teams from both sides started to lose interest in the merger. The board of management, which sustained its feeling that the merger was a good idea, called in reinforcements from outside to get the process back on track. Within eight weeks, the combined team worked out the most important synergies and laid down a solid base for the implementation of the merger. Enthusiasm for the merger was on the rise again throughout the organization.

This example highlights the price paid for getting bogged down in the analysis. Time, enthusiasm, and results all suffered. Percy Barnevik echoes those sentiments:

> 'I tell my people that if we make 100 decisions and 70 turn out to be right, that's good enough. I'd rather be roughly right and fast than exactly right and slow ... Why emphasize speed at the expense of precision? Because the costs of delay are vastly greater than the costs of an occasional mistake.'[26]

Make it a habit to analyze something once, and stick with that analysis until something very significant comes along to invalidate it. Streamline the process by keeping track of what you've analyzed and why you've rejected certain courses of action. That can be a real time saver when someone tries to resurrect a previously rejected idea. The facts are at hand to quickly cut the discussion and move forward.

Create decision-making highways

No successful company can exist without making decisions, easy ones as well as tough ones. There have to be decisions and they have to be communicated. They must be explicit, not implicit, in a restructuring plan. That involves identifying as far as possible which decisions will have to be made when, and making sure the relevant information is available within those deadlines so there is no excuse for delay.

Look at your company's track record in decision-making. What kinds of decisions usually take too long to make? What processes are considered too complicated? And are there areas where decisions are likely to be made without enough thought? Anticipating potential trouble spots ahead of time tells you where to watch during implementation.

The most important aspect of a decision-making highway is securing access to top management. Top management has to open its doors to key members of the restructuring team and be prepared to make decisions based on key information. Requirements for long and formal briefings have to fall away. Top management needs to have an atmosphere of open access, completely outside the regular business structure and free of bureaucracy. Many companies address this by scheduling a regular, say weekly, meeting between top management and the restructuring team. Even this is too rigid – if a decision needs to be made today, there should be a way of getting that decision immediately. Effective decision-making highways are key to getting a restructuring accomplished.

Set and sustain the cadence of restructuring

The prospect of recurring restructuring has a number of implications. First is the challenge of running restructuring and day-to-day operations simultaneously. Two very different activities that will demand executive attention at the same time. Second, if restructuring is truly continuous, one project will follow after another with no breathing space between. That means that the phenomenon of restructuring burn-out, or restructuring fatigue, evidenced in our survey (see Chapter 2), will become an even greater challenge. Restructurers pointed out that with each successive restructuring it was more difficult to get the workforce to buy in:

'This is the second such experience we have achieved – in the first, the attitudes were much better'

Employees complained of:

'too many restructuring programmes'

and asked,

'Is this the restructuring, or is there another one around the corner?'

Part of that attitude comes from past 'slash and burn' efforts, and from past failures. There's little incentive to get on board for yet another restructuring if you expect the result to be that you lose your job, or that the restructuring won't lead to any real improvement in the company's fortunes. But it also reflects a saturation point in the amount of change they (or any of us) can absorb.

Developing a cadence for restructuring may solve these problems. Establishing cadence means imposing a rhythm or cycle (see Figure 5.4). A new restructuring project will begin every x months, and will be completed y months before the next restructuring starts. If everyone in the company knows that's the pattern, expectations are set and planning occurs accordingly. Together with the Spearheaders, cadence is an important tool for being able to manage restructuring and day-to-day operations simultaneously. Imposing a cadence means setting up a process for restructuring, and it's that process that will enable top management to handle the dual challenges. Restructuring, even within business units, becomes a series of discrete projects, each completed while they're still relevant, with breathing space between that allows the organization to adapt to the new way of doing things and plan for the next effort.

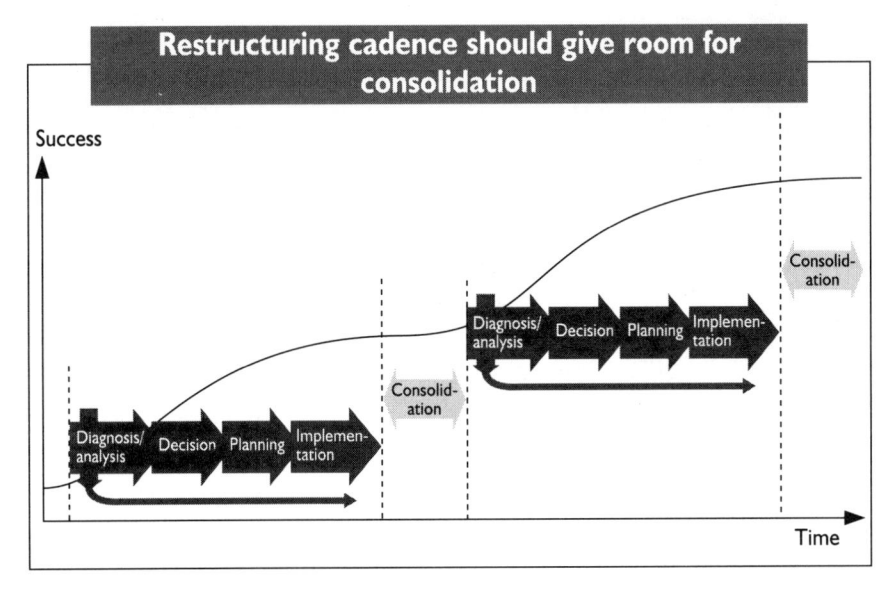

Figure 5.4

'Cadence' means thinking about restructuring in a new way. Theoretically holding to a strict cadence means identifying how much time there is for the restructuring and choosing projects that can be completed in that timeframe. First, figure out the appropriate length of time for making major changes (including an evaluation of how fast the organization can assimilate those changes) – this will become the restructuring cadence for the company. Restructuring projects should fit within that timeframe. In practice, market changes and business demands make fixed cadence difficult, but the goal of securing breathing space should be pursued nonetheless. Sometimes it can mean changing the scope of a project; sometimes it can mean adding resources.

Kvaerner

Kvaerner, the Norwegian shipbuilding, engineering and construction group, has incorporated the concept of cadence into its approach to restructuring. The company's different businesses regularly evaluate acquisition opportunities. Each acquisition they carry out is followed by a restructuring designed to integrate the new enterprise and capture the synergies the combined businesses offer. The companies make a point of taking a breath between these restructurings, to enable the changes to take root and to give the company time to examine and evaluate new opportunities.

The frequency of a company's restructuring cadence will be impacted by its restructuring experience. British Airways, for example, can move more quickly and restructure more frequently than Deutsche Bahn, partly because everyone is more used to the process.

Keep your eye on the ball

Tangible, sustainable results are the goal of any restructuring. There are a number of things you can do to make sure you get there.

Start with a stake in the ground: an overall long-term goal for achieving the broad restructuring objectives. For example, in a merger situation, the date by which the newly merged entity will be operational. That stake in the ground is a big picture goal which provides an overall target for the organization.

Within the broad framework of the stake in the ground, and before you start your restructuring, make sure that you have identified key, measurable deliverables for each project. Failure to specify measurable outcomes before the process starts is the primary block to successful, value-adding implementation. Concentrate on a few core deliverables rather than trying to identify everything. Take the time to think about what the key deliverable is for a specific project.

Within the frame of those tangible outputs, identify milestones that will tell whether the restructuring is on track to achieve its goals. Milestones are important for two reasons. They provide a target for a project team's activities, and they allow interested observers to see how a project is progressing. Milestones and deliverables have to be clearly specified so that it is easy to see whether or not they have been reached. Make them frequent enough, say monthly or quarterly, so that there's regular evidence of progress, and so that the restructuring can never get too far off track without someone noticing. Make sure that the milestones are clear indicators of progress. Tracking expenditures against budget, for example, would not be a good measure of progress. If you are overspending, it may leave the impression that the project is ahead of schedule, when in fact it may be behind schedule and well over budget.

Don't forget about the milestones and results for these new activities. The new ad campaign has been launched, but what should it deliver? How will you know if you're getting the results you want and need? Recognize two levels: the restructuring activity itself, and the new operations that result from that activity.

Prioritizing builds momentum

Restructuring is made up of a series of sub-projects, and proper sequencing of those sub-projects can have a significant impact on the success and speed of the overall restructuring (see Figure 5.5). The first look at priorities should consider three dimensions: the project's impact on the value of the restructuring; the time horizon of its impact; and its cost and resource requirements. The highest priority projects are those with the greatest value impact combined with the shortest time horizon. Among those, the preference is for those with the smallest investment. This prioritization can also help weed out low value projects: those with little value impact and very long time horizons are of least interest, and you should consider whether they are worth carrying out at all.

Prioritize project importance

Ease of implementation (High / Low) vs Time horizon (Short / Long)

- High priority sub-projects
- Sub-project A
- Sub-project B
- Sub-project C
- Sub-project D
- Low priority sub-projects

○ value impact

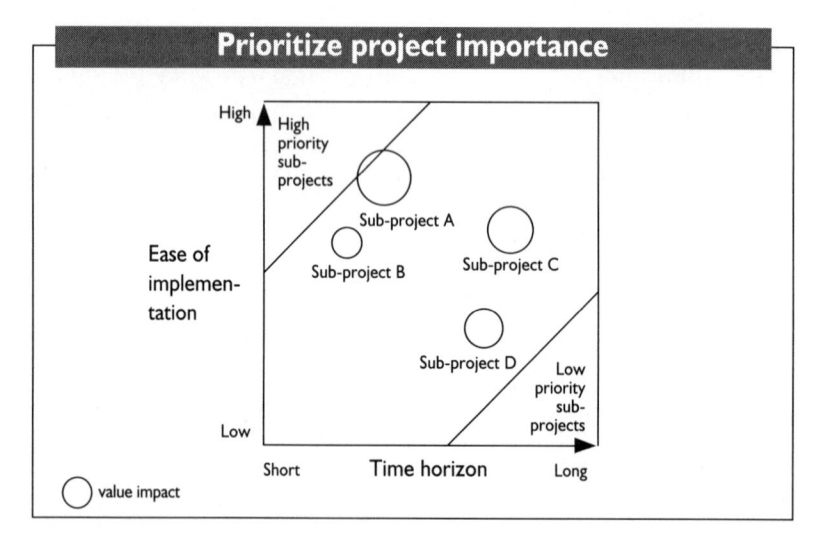

Figure 5.5

An additional dimension for prioritizing restructuring projects is the search for early wins. Restructurings, by virtue of their past pain and failure rates, will have many open and hidden sceptics. One or two early wins can do a lot to consolidate support and to prove to the doubters that the restructuring really is achievable and valuable. So overlay this question on the prioritization you have already done: which project is the easiest? And think back to your stakeholder analysis. Which stakeholders are you most concerned about winning over? That will direct you to projects that have the ability to consolidate the mindset in favour of the restructuring.

Employees are the most obvious group to consider. Early success in the restructuring process can go a long way towards convincing employees that the restructuring plan is a sound one and that they, together with the rest of the company, have what it takes to get the job done. This early proof of success reinforces, as well, the changed behaviours required during and after the restructuring. A powerful start to building the company's new way of doing things is proof that it works.

Early wins, however, need to be carefully managed. Don't let them turn into a signal for letting up. To reach the ambitious end goal, it's important to keep up the pressure and to make it clear that an early win is just that and nothing more. Our survey respondents warned of this danger: '*As soon as first results become visible, there's a risk that the development will stop*'. The following case study of an airline restructuring is an example of early wins being mistaken for complete victory.

Compromise

A European airline found itself losing money and losing ground, especially to its main competitor in its home country. Investigating the scope for cost reduction, they discovered that their pilots were earning salaries much higher than those in the other airlines. Senior management realized reducing salaries would be a difficult task, and indeed did run into serious problems. The result was a compromise between management and labour, with salaries not coming down as much as necessary to make the airline competitive. Both sides, however, considered the compromise a success, and considered this early victory a sign that the company's problems were solved. The restructuring was stopped at that point, the company soon fell behind again, and was forced into the difficult process of starting another restructuring after having declared its troubles over.

Turn an early win into a reason for becoming even more ambitious, instead of a signal for reducing the pressure. Once you have proved what your team can accomplish, build on it to secure further accomplishments. A European construction conglomerate took an interesting approach to building on its early wins:

Launch pad

The construction company was a full service one: design, build, and manage. It was looking to restructure the way it was carrying out its property and asset management, with a view to taking more responsibility for managing the total value of the asset rather than just taking care of the physical premises and collecting the rent. It meant a big change in the work that was carried out at each property, and to excel at this new approach it would become more important to share information across sites, rather than have each function completely independently. The company established confidence in the restructuring by starting its implementation at one site only. This let the kinks get worked out, and the first site became a role model and reference point for the other sites. Project managers saw that the system worked, and that there were tangible benefits to be achieved. And the precedent of information sharing that was started with the model site served as a launching pad for more and better communication among sites.

Consider interdependencies

The luxury of having only one thing going on at a time is rare. There are frequent problems in co-ordinating activities across different business units or different groups within a particular business unit.

> **Failure to co-ordinate across projects can hamper restructuring speed and success**
>
> *'Fixed structures at the interfaces to other divisions of the company make changes difficult.'*
>
> *'Restructuring in other business units impacted our restructuring process and there was a poor understanding of how the business unit interacts in the context of the corporation.'*

When setting priorities for restructuring activities, don't forget to look at the interdependencies. These can occur among restructuring projects or between restructuring projects and the company's current operations. Develop a critical path that details these interdependencies – which projects need to be done before others can be started? It isn't as simple as identifying whether one project's output forms the input for another project. The allocation of scarce resources is an important consideration as well. Maybe Project B can't be started, not because it needs the output of Project A, but because the person most critical to Project B is fully committed to Project A for the time being. This exercise will also highlight critical internal people and whether the demands on them are realistic or excessive: will it be necessary to bring in some outside resources?

This co-ordinating activity is on-going throughout the restructuring process. Expect some problems to arise, and watch to see whether inter-project dependency is a cause for slippage and delay during the implementation of the restructuring. Project groups tend to see their own goals as paramount, and it is important for the Spearheaders to make sure that a balanced view prevails. Review priorities regularly throughout the restructuring, to make sure that the focus is always on the most appropriate projects for the moment. Reprioritizing is necessary because circumstances can change, either externally or in the company's regular business operations. These changes can make the original priorities incorrect or no longer feasible. But the change in circumstances is a reason to reprioritize, not a reason to stop. Take this example from Rover:

Reprioritizing

Rover was in the midst of a complicated restructuring when they were acquired by BMW. The acquisition meant that all restructuring plans had to be reviewed and new priorities established, but it did not mean that the restructuring no longer had to happen. Rather, it meant that BMW got involved in the restructuring, adding its expertise and outside perspective to Rover's team.

The Spearheaders will always have an eye to the priorities and how they are set between restructuring and business as usual, between different restructuring projects, and between one business unit and other parts of the company. However, priorities are also likely to be adapted by others participating in the restructuring. That's a positive sign of the problem-solving, committed nature we want to foster in our employees. Nevertheless, the Spearheaders should keep close watch, without making their terms of reference so broad that they restrict projects. People have to feel like they have the power to decide their own destinies, and to believe that empowerment and taking responsibility for their own actions is real. A well-designed performance measurement system will help establish appropriate priorities across the group – more about this later.

When establishing priorities for projects, think about what you're asking of your people. The Spearheaders should be able to put themselves in the shoes of their people to understand what combination of projects will get the most out of the people and ensure their support throughout.

> **When establishing priorities for projects, think about what you're asking of your people.**

- Follow the early win with a more difficult project – alternate between challenging and less challenging projects, with each challenging project more so than the last.
- Don't run two tough sub-projects simultaneously, because people will rebel.
- Communicate clearly.
- Give your employees the chance to make decisions.

Use the early win as a stepping-stone to prove to the team that they can accomplish even more. Stretch them with a more difficult challenge, to build that confidence even further. We have found that people are sometimes scared when they come to realize their full potential, and that it makes them temporarily ultra cautious or unable to act.

Be careful about being too ambitious. The most common manifestation of that is trying to radically cut costs at the same time as you try to radically improve service. That's a recipe for overload. Instead, sequence these big gulps so that they occur one after the other. If cost-cutting is urgent, start with that and then work towards service improvement. What activity is most crucial to the survival of the company? That's the one to emphasize.

> ### Iberia Airlines and Alitalia
>
> Recent restructurings at both Iberia Airlines and Alitalia got stalled because the one-two punch of cost cutting and service improvement was launched simultaneously. It resulted in overload, and neither was accomplished as well as it could have been.

We've covered a number of dimensions to the issue of priority. How do you put it all together? The goal is to maximize results for a range of activities. Figure out what order brings the best results, both in absolute terms and with regard to the probability of success. That's one of the key jobs for the Spearheaders.

Choose the implementation sequence which:

- delivers the fastest achievement of benefits
- minimizes the use of additional funding
- minimizes resource conflicts
- does the best job of minimizing inter-project dependencies
- builds confidence and enthusiasm among stakeholders, especially employees

---

Performance measurement guides activity

Performance measurement plays a critical role in encouraging people to stay focused and work on activities that are relevant to the company's goals. We emphasize, again, that in order for performance measurement to be an effective tool, it *must* relate the performance measurement to the results the company is looking for. If it is critical that the various restructuring teams interact and benefit from each other's input, for example, make part of the reward system dependent on overall results that can only be achieved with that co-operation. Simplicity should be a goal. Performance measurement systems should help people direct their attention, but if the system is too complicated it won't achieve that goal.

> **Siemens**
>
> Siemens is a good example of a company that has learned to tailor its performance measurement systems to the goal it wants to achieve. Because it needs to be able to raise equity financing, the company is putting extra emphasis on profits these days. That's reflected in performance measurements in a number of ways. First, Siemens' top 150 managers can now double their income through the performance of the businesses they run. Siemens also reports its profitability to the outside world by business segment. That increases the pressure on poorly performing businesses to pick up their socks. And business segments are now measured in terms of value creation – that's a real departure for Siemens, where the emphasis used to be more on sales growth than earnings growth.

Another company had to learn the hard way:

> **Service company**
>
> A professional service company whose number one goal was high speed growth got caught in a fight for savings that stifled growth and caused some years of missed growth targets. A new chief controller discovered that management was measured against its contribution to bottom line savings and not in terms of growth. This rule changed, growth milestones were communicated and finally the company started growing at a higher rate.

Keep watching the sensor screen

We've talked about how a good sensor system can help direct the company towards an appropriate strategy, and help pinpoint when changes in strategy are needed (see page 132). The second function of the sensor system is to look for inconsistencies during the implementation of restructuring. Are things proceeding according to plan? The sensor system watches out for unexpected developments. It looks for mismatches between strategy and action; between performance measures and the actions that are needed to achieve desired results; between what top management believes is happening and employees' interpretation of the same thing. Companies need to collect information that is relevant and current so that they can tell when problems are arising.

Information system

A European manufacturer with global interests built an information system that gave it a competitive edge. Sitting at a desk in Europe, the chief of production can check on information from around the world: productivity in Eastern Europe; sales in the Far East; shipments to Mexico.

The ability to instantly access last night's operating figures, instead of last month's, pinpoints pressing issues quickly and effectively.

A sensor system's effectiveness is enhanced by good communication. Employees who know what's expected can do a better job of pointing out discrepancies between expectations and reality. But it's the communication in the other direction that can have the most substantial impact. Our suspicion is that the information-gathering part of the sensor system already exists in most companies. Ask any employee what's going right or wrong with the business, and they'll usually have an answer of some relevance. They'll tell you something you didn't know but wished you had. Your job is to search out that information.

IN BRIEF

Orchestrating

- Spearheaders who as a group cover all leadership attributes drive implementation and ensure employee involvement.

- Finding the appropriate rhythm for frequent restructurings is the pathway to market dominance: develop an individual cadence that makes it possible for leaders and Spearheaders to lean back and be creative about new possibilities.

6

Towards the future

There is one!

Que será, será – whatever will be, will be ...

Complacency is a tough word, but it fits Europe much better than any other characteristic in this day and age. Complacency is not only what companies on all levels suffer from, it is also a common denominator from a political perspective. Indicators are heard and seen everywhere:

> **Continental Europe has not yet discovered its role in the 21st century.**

- *Exports are still our core strength. We export world champions.*

  But: will this still hold true in the face of the Asian crisis? Will that enormous customer potential break away in the very short term? And will that not lead to even tougher competitive pressure from Asia?

- *Economies are actually growing and will even revive with the ECU just around the corner.*

  But: nothing will take a turn for the better in countries like France, Germany or Italy, as long as tax and labour laws are what they are.

- *Monopolies – often breeding grounds for complacency – are on the way out. Deregulation, such as in the telecoms industry, will lead to increasing competition and more dynamic business.*

  But: this or any other monopoly is most likely to come back in through the back door. Intensified cycles of restructuring will not only trigger shake-outs and concentration, but eventually, will also help to build up new monopolies.

In short, even though some visionary entrepreneurs have understood what has to be done, Europe still does not fully grasp the shifts economies are currently undergoing. Continental Europe has not yet discovered its role in the 21st century.

While all this is gradually becoming common knowledge and

creating a sense of urgency, there are other voices telling quite a different story. These voices are maybe not as loud but they're worth listening to. They talk about what has been accomplished. And there definitely are achievements. Europe has become more of a reality during the last couple of years, as people and governments realize they can become European without abandoning their national identities. And this *status quo* could well become protection against competitive challenges from Asia or the US. Moreover, Europe's diversity and pluralism are a dream come true, while the economic system is stable and relatively harmonious. All this is the result of reconciliation as well as increasing co-operation. It sends signals to those still lagging behind in terms of democracy and negotiation-based political decisions, not just in the Balkans, but also in Asia.

In short we are not doing badly, but we could do much better. We should aim for a prospering European economy, like the one we are watching with envy in the US right now, where unemployment has nearly vanished, growth rates are outstanding and the president, who made this turnaround a reality, now has a greater degree of freedom than any of his predecessors ever had.

European politicians are now discussing the overwhelming problem of creating new jobs and securing the old ones but they're stuck in a vicious circle. As long as taxes are high, small and medium-sized companies will have to be extremely careful when adding new staff (they opt for extensive overtime by existing employees instead), and as long as people are not willing (and sometimes not able) to work for less, there will be no incentive to stop the overtime tradition. Additionally, given the high allowances for the unemployed, the only job market that corresponds to supply and demand is the dark grey market of hundreds of thousands of handymen, housekeepers, babysitters, interior decorators, etc.

Experts are beginning to realize that breaking this vicious circle is the most important issue at stake, and that means addressing the structural origin of European unemployment. So far Europe hasn't done the job. But there is hope – in a very silent but effective mode – the Dutch have succeeded in changing their economy to create jobs on a sustained basis. Even after attaining an unemployment rate of about 5%, which is sensational compared to rates in most other European countries (mostly more than 10%), the Dutch are now working on tax cuts to improve the economy even further. One focus will be to reduce significantly value added tax on labour-intensive services, a move that will be likely to cut into the black market, and probably also trigger the development of a more service-oriented economy similar to that in the US today.

Politics can also prove beneficial in other ways:

- improving conditions for mobility, by not taxing relocation allowances
- relieving the tax load of small and medium-sized companies
- fostering qualification initiatives
- re-engineering political decision processes to safeguard both the market economy and the social safety net.

Reducing State involvement in the economies has benefited many countries worldwide. It should also be a model for Europe.

The numbers look promising in 1998. Britain and the Netherlands have achieved low unemployment rates without resulting inflation. Growth is the only way out for other more politically rigid countries – with all the possible implications.

What does this mean for companies all over Europe? There is no reason to be complacent and wait for the State or the European Union to create more favourable conditions for their businesses. Instead, top managers should learn from the lessons successful companies have taught them – many of which are to be found in this book – and become not just controllers, but entrepreneurs in the truest sense of the word.

References

1. Thomas R. Horton, *The CEO Paradox. The Privilege and Accountability of Leadership*, 1991, p. 129.
2. Noel M. Tichy and Mary Anne Devanna, *The Transformational Leader*, 1986, p.77.
3. Richard House, 'Philippe Jaffré's un-French revolution', *Institutional Investor*, July 1997, pp. 60–66.
4. The Economist Intelligence Unit, *Developing Leadership for the 21st Century*, 1996.
5. Roger Cohen, 'A somber France, racked by doubt', *International Herald Tribune*, 1997.
6. Edward Carr, 'A fortress against change', *The Economist*, November 23, 1996.
7. Eli Cohen and Noel Tichy, 'How leaders develop leaders', *Training and Development*, May 1997, p. 65.
8. See note [6].
9. 'Furnishing the world', *The Economist*, November 19, 1994, p. 83.
10. William Taylor, 'The logic of global business: an interview with ABB's Percy Barnevik', *Leaders on Leadership*, 1992, pp. 67–90.
11. See note [6].
12. See note [10].
13. Charles Heckscher, *White-Collar Blues. Management Loyalties in an Age of Corporate Restructuring*, 1995.
14. Dr. R. Morgan Gould, *Revolution at Oticon A/S*, IMD case OB235, 1994.
15. 'Corporate surveys can't find a productivity revolution either', *Challenge*, Nov.–Dec. 1995, p. 31.
16. A. Bennett, 'Management: downsizing does not necessarily bring an upswing corporate profitability', *Wall Street Journal*, June 6, 1991, p. 13.
17. Hermann Simon, *Hidden Champions: Lessons from 500 of the World's Best Companies*, 1996, pp. 53–54.
18. Matthew J. Kieman, *Set Innovative or Sethead*, 1995, pp. 160–63.
19. Professors Tom Vollmann and Carlos Cordon, Jussi Heikkila, *Skanska and Rockwool: Making the Supply Chain Partnership work*, IMD case POM 184, 1996.
20. W. Chan Kim and Renee Mauborgne, 'Opportunity beckons', *Financial Times*, August 18, 1997.

21 Thomas Hout, Michael E. Porter and Eileen Rudden, 'How global companies win out', *Global Strategies*, 1994, pp. 35–36.
22 See note [19].
23 Kees van der Heijden, *Scenario Building*, 1996, pp. 15–22.
24 Greg Steinmetz, 'Siemens discovers a new raison d'être: to make profits', *Wall Street Journal*, February 19, 1998.
25 David Owen, 'French sell-offs back on track', *Financial Times*, September 6, 1997.
26 See note [10].

Index

Index entries are to page numbers, those in italic referring to figures.

3M	55
ABB	49, 59, 82
acceptance	5
and enthusiasm, matrix	63
lacking	62
achievements	
rewarding	73–6
standards	73
acquisitions	17, 18, 23
action	137
cadence of restructuring, setting and sustaining	156–8
consolidation	*157*
companies poised for	55–8
goals, achieving	
co-ordinating activities	163–6
cost requirements	160
deliverables	159
early wins	161–2
employees, early wins encouraging	161
interdependencies	163–6
interproject dependencies	164
launch pads	162–3
milestones	159–60
performance measurement guiding activity	166–7
prioritizing	160–3, 163–6
reprioritizing	164
resource requirements	160
sensor systems	168
stakeholders, encouraging	161
time horizon of impact	160
value, impact of projects on	160
Spearheaders as frontmen	138–9
speed	149–51, *149*
analyzing properly	154–5
decision making	152–3

Index

highways, creation	155
delays	152–3, *153*
top management, access to	155
stakeholders	
classification of	139–40
communication	146–9
co-ordination of responsibilities	146
employees	142–3
capabilities	144–5
credibility	144
salesforce evaluation	145
external	147–8
governments	147–8
internal	140
early involvement	142–3
middle management, exclusion of	143
negotiating with	141
objectives of	141
orienting	139–41
resources, availability of	143–6
segmentation	147
skills, availability of	143–6
suppliers	140
undivided attention	22, *138*
action–orientation	60
Adtranz	114
AEG	30, 49
AGIV	15
Ahold	3, 119–20, 121, 125
Air France	148
Airbus Industrie	53, 61, 82
Alitalia	166
alliances	17–18, *19*
analyzing properly	154–5
Ansaldo	15
anticipating change	53–5
AO Volga	120
arrogance	5, 48–9
Austria	154
automotive industry	17
suppliers, recognizing and managing	140
balance	36–8
balanced scorecard	74

Index

Barnevik, Percy	59, 70, 108, 154
BASF	15
Bayer	15
Belgium	
cinema industry	122
believers	33–5
benchmarking	65–6
as imposter for strategy	100–1
Bert Claeys	122
Bertelsmann	34
Blanc, Christian	61, 148
blocking restructuring	43
BMW	164
boards of directors *see* top management	
Bobeck, Manfred	105–6
Boeing	53, 61
Borealis	18
Boston Consulting matrix	127
BP	3
BPR *see* business process re–engineering	
Brabeck, Peter	50
Branson, Richard	78
breathing space	10, *157*
British Airways	7, 158
culture change	81
proactive approach	53
vision	95
broad–mindedness	36–8
budgeting	
as imposter for strategy	102–3
building companies poised for action	55–8
business cultures	29
business expansion	23
business process re–engineering	
as imposter for strategy	101
cadence of restructuring	10
setting and sustaining	156–8
Carrefour	3
change	
expectation of, nurturing	76–7
recognizing need for	54
chemical industry	113
chief executives *see* top management	

181

Index

Chirac, Jacques	61
choices, unwillingness to make	108
cinema industry, Belgium	122
Citibank	113
closing capacity	23
co–operation	113
co–ordinating activities	163–6
co–ordination of responsibilities	146
commitment	
and compliance, difference between	67
lacking when targets imposed	64
leadership	29–30
top management	19–20
commodity type industries	
cost leadership	112–13
communication	6
in context accessible for employees	71
effectiveness, evaluating	72
with employees	71
feedback from	71–2
fostering winning mindset	67–72
lack of	20
problems	31
stakeholders	146–9
top management	61
transparency	72
two–way	72
competencies, strengthening	104
competition	
for customers	130, *130*
experts from	65
for investment	130, *130*
for resources	130, *130*
competitive changes	
anticipating or creating	54
competitive drives	
balancing to gain buy–in	129–32
competition for customers	130, *130*
competition for investment	130, *130*
competition for resources	130, *130*
post–merger situations	131–2
competitors	
differentiating from	98
experts from	65

understanding	109
complacency	4, 5, 29, 45–6
Europe	173–5
example	67
fighting	64
German machinery industry	46
Royal Dutch Shell	47–8
stamping out	47
compliance	64
and commitment, difference between	67
compromise	162
computer industry	98
confusion	132
consolidation between restructurings	157
cost	24
focus on	73, 74
cost control	
strategy	117
cost–cutting	49
as imposter for strategy	102
strategy	88–9, 117
cost leadership	8, 73–4
constant challenge	111–15
European companies, feasibility for	114–15
innovations	115
locational advantages	114
strategy	98, 104
value leadership	111
cost obsession	73–4
cost–orientation	21
cost requirements	160
courage	
to choose	104–11
lack of	59
results–orientated decisions	59–60
credibility	
employees	144
Spearheaders	41–2
crisis situations	53, 89–90, 124
cultural barriers	29
cultural rigidity	57
culture	
evolving	78–82
national	81–2

Index

regional	81–2
curiosity	58
customer orientation	107, 109
customers	
competition for	130, *130*
importance of strategy to	98–9
joint competencies with	17
needs	111
strategy for growth	121
Daimler–Benz	8, 49, 50, 107–8
data mining	123
DB AG (Deutsche Bahn AG)	107, 158
de Saint–Exupéry, Antoine	91
decision making	9–10, 152–3
employee involvement	23
highways, creation	155
results orientation	59–60
toughness	37–8
decisiveness	36–8
delays	152–3, *153*
deliverables	159
Delony	152
Denmark	60–1
Deutsche Bahn AG	107, 158
development of strategy *see* strategy	
differentiating from competitors	98
directors *see* top management	
Dormann, Jürgen	75
Dornier	49
downsizing	
middle management reaction to	76–7
strategy	88, 102, 117–18
Du Pont de Nemours	15
early wins	161–2
EDI (Electronic Data Interchange)	123
effectiveness	
of communication, evaluating	72
elective restructuring	89–91, *90*
Electronic Data Interchange (EDI)	123
Elektro BAU AG	20
Elf Aquitaine	36, 61
ELIN EBG	20
emergency restructuring	89–91, *90*

Index

employees	
capabilities	144–5
communication in context accessible for	71
communication with	71
credibility	144
early wins encouraging	161
enthusiasm	5
involvement	23, 142–3
limited access to information	70
perspective	71
resistance	29
restructuring, views on	58
restructuring obstacles	19, 20
salesforce evaluation	145
valuable contributions	69
Endesa	116
enthusiasm	5
and acceptance, matrix	63
lacking	62
top management	61
Ericsson, L.M.	123, 145
ethnic cultures	29
Europe	
co–operation	174
complacency	173–5
diversity	174
economic system	174
industrial traditions	52
market economy	175
pluralism	174
reconciliation	174
unemployment	174–5
European companies	
cost leadership, feasibility of	114–15
global competition, vulnerability to	3
success	3
European survey of restructuring	3–4
expectations of restructuring	15–16, *16*
experience	
Spearheaders	42
experts	
from competitors	65
Spearheaders	40–1
external stakeholders	147–8

Index

facts	
interpreting	122
failure	
tolerating	77–8
feedback	36
from communication	71–2
stakeholders	138–9
Fiat	15
financial services industry	113
FitzGerald, Niall	22
flexibility	58
focus	21, 23–4
arguments against	111
competitors, understanding	109
concentration of resources	104
on cost	73, 74
courage to choose	104–11
customer needs	111
customer orientation	107, 109
focused differentiation	98, 104–11
strategy	8
strengthening competencies	104
value migration, identifying	109
focused differentiation	98, 104–11
Fokker	49
following up all opportunities	
as imposter for strategy	103
forward–thinkers	
Spearheaders	42
France	36, 147–8, 173
frequency of restructuring	15–16
front lines, reliance on	56
General Electronic	140
Germany	173
machinery industry	46
Glaxo Wellcome	116
globalization	16–17, 17, 23
goals, achieving *see* action	
governments as stakeholders	147–8
growth	
restructuring for	3
strategy for *see* strategy	
growth orientation	21, 23–4

Index

Guinness/Grand Metropolitan	82
Hayek, Nicholas	100
Herlitz, Peter	120
Herlitz International Trading	120
high expectations	
top management	61
Hoechst	75
Hoesch AG	66
Hoeven, Cees van der	119
Iberia Airlines	166
IKEA	57
implementation	
challenge	9
employee involvement	23
imposters for strategy *see* strategy: setting	
improvement programmes	55
inertia	4, 5, 29, 45–8
inflexibility	56
information	
employees' limited access to	70
as power	71
ready communication of	70
stakeholders	138–9
see also communication	
information systems	168
innovations, cost leadership	115
interdependencies	17–18, 163–6
internal stakeholders	140
early involvement	142–3
interpreting facts	122
interproject dependencies	164
investment	
competition for	130, *130*
Italy	173
Jaffré, Philippe	36, 61
joint competencies with suppliers and customers	17
joint ventures	17, 23
Klöckner Humboldt Deutz	66
Koninklijke Ahold *see* Ahold	
Kvaerner	10, 158

187

Index

L'Oréal	116
launch pads	162–3
leaders	
believers	33–5
consistency between saying and doing	33
recipients of market and company signals	51
setting tone	33
success or failure	31–2
tough decisions	37–8
see also Spearheaders	
leadership	5
commitment	29–30
by example	34
issues	32
living	33
responsibilities	32
leading companies' change in mindset	31–44
learning	58
learning from experience	15
the best and the rest	21
focus	21, 23–4
growth orientation	21, 23–4
new management	24–5
speed	21–3
future restructuring	
frequency	15–16
globalization	16–17, *17*
interdependence	17–18
lessons from the past	19–21
Leschly, Jan	36
lessons from the past	19–21
locational advantages, cost leadership	114
MacDonnell Douglas	53
Major, John	32
management *see* middle management; new management; top management	
Marchés Usines Auchan	116
market shifts	
anticipating or creating	54
marketing prospects	
and vision	95–6
Marshall, Sir Colin	53
mavericks, making room for	77–8

Index

McKinsey Seven S framework	127
measurement *see* performance measurement	
mergers	18, *19*
Metallgesellschaft	66
middle management	
downsizing, reactions to	76–7
exclusion of	143
resistance	29, 30
restructuring, reactions to	76–7
milestones	159–60
misinformation	132
Moberg, Anders	57
mobilizing organization	39–40
monopolies	173
motor industry *see* automotive industry	
Motorola	145
national cultures	81–2
Nesté	18
Nestlé	50
Netherlands	60, 119, 125, 132, 174
Neukirchen, Kajo	66
new industry, dissecting	123
new management	24–5, *24*, 49–50, 65
new market opportunities	23
new potential	
unearthing	49–52
Nokia	110, 145
North America	
competition with	3
progress	3
Ollila, Jorma	110
open–mindedness	50–1, *51*
top management	61
vision	97
openness	50
opportunities, sensor systems for	132–3
option generation	
employee involvement	23
orchestrating *see* action	
Oticon	79–80
outdated strategy, reliance on	
as imposter for strategy	99–100

Index

outsiders' views	63–7
people issues *see* employees	
performance expectations	73–6
performance measurement	73
guiding activity	166–7
simplicity	166–7
Spearheaders	44
Pfleiderer	64
Philip Morris Europe	15
Philips	64
Pierer, Heinrich von	57
poor communications	30
portfolio planning	127
position power	
Spearheaders	40
post–merger situations	
competitive drives	131–2
integration	20
potential for growth	118–24
price performance	151
prioritizing	160–3, 163–6
privatization	68, 79, 148
proactive restructuring	54, 89, 124, *125*
problem definition	
employee involvement	23
productivity improvement	49
profitable lines of business	121
Promodès	116
reactive restructuring	54, 89
real growth	116
redefining the industry	125
refocusing	22
regional cultures	81–2
relevance *see* strategy	
reprioritizing	164
resources	
availability of	143–6
competition for	130, *130*
concentration of	104
requirements	160
responsiveness to new ideas	50
restructuring	

concepts of	4–5
elective	89–91, *90*
emergency	89–91, *90*
European survey of	3–4, 15
growth	3
mindset for	4–6
nature and meaning	89
proactive	54, 89, 124, *125*
reactive	54, 89
success	11
Restructuring Affinity Council	4
restructuring paralysis	152
results–oriented decisions	59–60
Reuter, Edzard	49
rewarding achievements	73–6
rigidity	56
cultural	57
Roche	3
role models	33–6
Rover	164
Royal Dutch/Shell	82
fighting complacency	47–8
scenario building	127–8
Saatchi & Saatchi	131
Saint–Exupéry, Antoine de	91
sales people	
capitalizing on knowledge of	56
salesforce evaluation	145
scenario building	127–8
Schrempp, Jürgen	49, 50, 108
Senge, Peter	128
sensor systems	168
for threats and opportunities	132–3
setting strategy *see* strategy	
share options	76
Shell *see* Royal Dutch/Shell	
short–term orientation	108, 117–18
Siemens	57, 140
performance measurement	167
simplicity	79
Skanska	111–12, 126
skills, availability of	143–6
'slash and burn' restructurings	29

Index

SmithKline Beecham	36
Spearheaders	30, 38–9
attributes	*41*
credibility	41–2
experience	42
experts	40–1
forward–thinkers	42
as frontmen	138–9
implementation	9
measuring performance	44
mobilizing organization	39–40
position power members	40
rewards matching performance	44
selection	6
setting pace	39–40
targeting, training and motivating	40–4
speed	21–3
see also action	
stakeholders	
classification of	139–40
communication	146–9
co-ordination of responsibilities	146
employees	142–3
capabilities	144–5
credibility	144
salesforce evaluation	145
encouraging	161
external	147–8
governments	147–8
internal	140
early involvement	142–3
involvement	9
middle management, exclusion of	143
negotiating with	141
objectives of	141
orienting	139–41
resources, availability of	143–6
segmentation	147
skills, availability of	143–6
suppliers	140
winning over	161
Statoil	18
Stet	150
strategic dynamics	128–9

Index

strategic gameboard	127
strategy	7–8
cost control	117
cost–cutting	88–9, 117
cost leadership	98, 104
see also setting *below*	
customers, importance to	98–9
by default	103
development	87
impeding	*109*
short–term orientation	108
downsizing	88, 102, 117–18
growth	8
challenge for	116
conditions for, preparing	124–6
customer needs	121
data mining	123
interpreting facts	122
inward, looking	121–2
new industry, dissecting	123
only option	117–18
outward, looking	121–2
potential	118–24
profitable and unprofitable lines of business	121
real	116
redefining the industry	125
short–term orientation	117–18
technological breakthroughs, dissecting	123
relevance	126
competitive drives	
balancing to gain buy–in	129–32
competition for customers	130, *130*
competition for investment	130, *130*
competition for resources	130, *130*
post–merger situations	131–2
sensor systems for threats and opportunities	132–3
testing strategy for outcomes	
Boston Consulting matrix	127
McKinsey Seven S framework	127
portfolio planning	127
scenario building	127–8
strategic dynamics	128–9
strategic gameboard	127
value chain analysis	127

Index

restructuring, connection with	89
setting	97–9
cost leadership	
constant challenge	111–15
European companies, feasibility for	114–15
innovations	115
locational advantages	114
value leadership	111
focus	
arguments against	111
competitors, understanding	109
concentration of resources	104
courage to choose	104–11
customer needs	111
customer orientation	107, 109
focused differentiation	98, 104–11
strengthening competencies	104
value migration, identifying	109
imposters	99
acceptance as replacement for true strategy	103
benchmarking	100–1
budgeting	102–3
business process re–engineering	101
cost–cutting	102
following up all opportunities	103
reliance on outdated strategy	99–100
vagueness	103
vision	91–3
compelling, building	96–7
developing	96–7
good and bad	93–6
leading strategy	93
marketing prospects	95–6
responsibility for developing	97
success	11
suppliers	
joint competencies with	17
recognizing and managing	140
survival	124
Swatch	100
Sweden	123, 126, 129
Switzerland	132
watch industry	100
systems dynamics	128

Index

technological breakthroughs, dissecting	123
technology development, rapidity	151
Telecom Italia	150
Telefónica	150
testing strategy for outcomes *see* strategy: relevance	
threats, sensor systems for	132–3
Thyssen	15
time horizon of impact	160
toleration	67
top management	
access to	155
commitment	19–20
communication	61
discrepancy between saying and doing	35, 73
see also leaders; leadership	
transparency	72
two–way communication	72
undivided attention	22, 138
unemployment	174–5
unfocused business approach	105
Unilever	3, 22, 82
United Kingdom	175
unprofitable lines of business	121
unwillingness to make choices	108
Usinor Sacilor	61
value, impact of projects on	160
value chain analysis	127
value leadership	111
value migration, identifying	109
van der Hoeven, Cees	119
VEBA	15
vision	91–3
compelling, building	96–7
developing	96–7
good and bad	93–6
leading strategy	93
marketing prospects	95–6
responsibility for developing	97
Volga	120
von Pierer, Heinrich	57
watch industry, Switzerland	100

Index

Welch, Jack	140
winning mindset	4–6, 29–31
challenging enemies of	44–5
anticipating change	53–5
arrogance	48–9
building companies poised for action	55–8
complacency and inertia	45–8
results–oriented decisions	59–60
unearthing new potential	49–52
fostering	60–3
communication	67–72
culture, evolving	78–82
expectation of change, nurturing	76–7
mavericks, making room for	77–8
outsiders' views	63–7
performance expectations	73–6
rewarding achievements	73–6
leading companies' change in mindset	31–2
broad–mindedness, balance and decisiveness	36–8
role models	33–6
Spearheaders	38–9
setting pace	39–40
targeting, training and motivating	40–4
Winterhalter Gastronom	105–6, 115
Wössner, Mark	34